The media's watch
Here's a sampling of our coverage.

"For those hoping to climb the ladder of success, [Vault's] insights are priceless."
– ***Money magazine***

"The best place on the web to prepare for a job search."
– ***Fortune***

"[Vault guides] make for excellent starting points for job hunters and should be purchased by academic libraries for their career sections [and] university career centers."
– ***Library Journal***

"The granddaddy of worker sites."
– ***U.S. News and World Report***

"A killer app."
– ***New York Times***

One of Forbes' 33 "Favorite Sites"
– ***Forbes***

"To get the unvarnished scoop, check out Vault."
– ***Smart Money Magazine***

"Vault has a wealth of information about major employers and job-searching strategies as well as comments from workers about their experiences at specific companies."
– ***The Washington Post***

"Vault has become the go-to source for career preparation."
– ***Crain's New York Business***

"Vault [provides] the skinny on working conditions at all kinds of companies from current and former employees."
– ***USA Today***

VAULT INSIDER GUIDE TO MEDICAL SCHOOL ADMISSIONS

VAULT INSIDER GUIDE TO MEDICAL SCHOOL ADMISSIONS

THE DUKE MEDICAL SCHOOL CLASS OF 2006
COORDINATED BY SUJAY KANSAGRA,
CLASS PRESIDENT

Library of Congress CIP Data is available.

ISBN 13: **978-1-58131-451-9**

ISBN 10: **1-58131-451-5**

Printed in the United States of America

ACKNOWLEDGMENTS

Acknowledgments from Sujay Kansagra and the Duke Medical School Class of 2006:

This work could not have been possible without the diligence and dedication of its 74 authors. They truly epitomize what it means to work together as a "Duke Med Family."

Harold Agbahiwe
Robert Angelo
Emma Archibong
Dustyn Baker
Priya Batra
Michele Blank
Willem Bok
Ebony Boyce
Molly Boyce
Malinda Boyd
Dana Cairo
Yolanda Chik
Emily Choi
Gabe Chong
Jessica Chow
Melissa Chung
Char DeCroos
Noelle DeSimone
Vikram Devisetty
Emily Eads
Nancy Edwards
David Evans
Sarah Evans
Parvin Fatheddin
Maheer Gandhavadi
Adepeju Gbadebo
Robi Goswami
Rachel Grisham
Christiane Haeffele
Nabeel Hamoui
Neil Hanson
Susan Harley
Sarah Hart
Andrea Havens
Chad Hembree
Jim Hotaling
Gabe Howles-Banerji
Kelley Hutcheson
Allen Hwang
Peter Jones
Sujay Kansagra
Prateeti Khazanie
Eugene Kim
Kara King
Jason Langheier
Thomas LeBlanc
Jeanne Lee
Aaron Lesher
Meghan Liel
Arwen Long
Michael Malinzak
Nathan Mall
Mark Neely
Ivana Nikolic
Stephen Odaibo
Lauren Parks
Sarita Patil
Srinivas Peddi
Thomas Petersen
Brooke Rosonke
Claire Sandstrom
Shervin Shirvani
Stanton Stebbins
Erica Taylor
Crystal Tung
Sarah Tyler
Joshua Unger
Jesse Waggoner
Kitch Wilson
Jeremy Wingard
Ayaba Worjoloh
Arthur Wu
Hui Xue
Qinghong Yang

Vault's acknowledgments:

We are extremely grateful to Vault's entire staff for all their help in the editorial, production and marketing processes. Vault also would like to acknowledge the support of our investors, clients, employees, family, and friends. Thank you!

Table of Contents

Chapter 8: Financial Aid and Scholarships 103

Chapter 9: Choosing a Medical School 113

OTHER CONSIDERATIONS 129

Chapter 10: The Nontraditional Applicant 131

Chapter 11: The Gap Year 147

Introduction

Preface

"I wish I had known that before I began." It is an almost inevitable thought after completing the medical school application process. It is our hope that you will never have to utter these words when it comes to your pre-medical experience. Over 70 members of the Duke Medical School Class of 2006 have collaborated to put together a book detailing the process from a diversity of angles. We will offer you insights into the things that worked well and the things that did not. We represent over 30 different states and three countries. And as group, we have applied to medical schools all around the country. Here's your chance to peek inside the lives of medical students who were in your shoes not long ago.

There is no such thing as the stereotypical medical school student. Thus, there is no one particular path that guarantees acceptance. Although there may be things you can do to better your chances of admission, there are no guarantees or definites. Keep this in mind when beginning your pre-medical experience in college. Your journey through the process will be like no other applicant, and that is the way it should be.

Since we do believe that each applicant is different from the rest, this book will attempt to show you the many options and opportunities available. It is up to you to choose your own path. We are here to ensure you know of the various forks in the road.

Each section will take you through parts of the process, including choosing a major, carrying out undergraduate research, participating in extracurricular activities, taking the MCAT, applying, interviewing and much more. Each chapter will address the basic facts you should know regarding each topic. After we have laid down the facts behind each step, we will offer you insight into how different classmates went through these individual steps. Along the way, we will show you the mistakes we have made, the options that lie before you, and of course, the things we wish we had known before it all began.

Best of luck in your endeavors!
Sujay Kansagra
President, Duke Medical School Class of 2006

The History of Medical Schools in the United States

The very first medical school in the original 13 colonies was founded in 1765 by John Morgan at the University of Pennsylvania, which at the time was known as the College of Philadelphia. The faculty had been trained at the University of Edinburgh and used British medical education as the model. Thus, the first medical school in the United States was built within an institution of higher learning. It promoted bedside learning that was to supplement medical lectures. The medical school was within a few blocks from the Pennsylvania Hospital that was founded by Benjamin Franklin.

Medical education in that era included formal lectures for a semester or two and several years of apprenticeship. There was no formal tuition, no prerequisite academic preparation and written exams were not mandatory. With the progress of science in the 19th Century started the new era of medical education calling for full-time investigators and teachers in biochemistry, bacteriology, pharmacology, etc. In the 1870s, the first teaching hospital, the Hospital of the University of Pennsylvania, was built. Teaching hospitals are those that teach future physicians the art of medicine, and thus have residents and medical students working alongside the main doctors (known as attendings).

Medical school in the 20th Century

The birth of modern medical education in the United States and Canada is often attributed to Abraham Flexner, a professional educator, who in 1910 published the Flexner Report for the Carnegie Foundation. The report was a commentary of the state of medical education at the time. It criticized the fact that there were too many medical schools, many of which were substandard. At the time the report was published there were 155 medical schools in the United States and Canada and only 16 of these required two or more years of college work as an admission requirement. (Many of the others came into being simply to make money from tuition as opposed to actually providing a quality education.) Flexner proposed a four-year medical school curriculum—two years of basic science education followed by two years of clinical training. He also proposed the requirements for admission to include the high school diploma and a minimum of two years of college science. The report resulted in the closure of many medical schools that were not incorporated within a university; this way, medical education would be associated with institutions known for academic excellence. In 1935 there were 66 MD granting institutions that survived the reform, 57 of which were part of a university.

These improvements in medical education were followed by the birth of standardized testing for medical school admissions. The Medical College Admission Test (MCAT) was developed in 1928. It was implemented to improve attrition rates that at the time ranged from 5 to 50 percent. By 1946 attrition rates at medical schools in the U.S. decreased to 7 percent.

The student body

As for the student body in these early medical schools, it will come as no surprise that the students were white and male. Medical schools were closed to African-Americans, except for a few older medical schools in the north. The first African-American to graduate from a northern medical school was Dr. David J. Peck, who graduated from Rush Medical School in Chicago in 1847. Between 1868 and 1904 seven medical schools for African-Americans were established. Unfortunately, by 1923 only Howard University Medical School in Washington and Meharry Medical School in Nashville remained open. Things were not much better for women. The first medical school for women, The Women's Medical College of Pennsylvania, was founded in 1850, and eventually came to be known as the Medical College of Pennsylvania. Drexel University eventually took over the school, and it is now known as Drexel College of Medicine. The first woman to graduate from a medical school in the U.S. was Dr. Elizabeth Blackwell. She graduated first in class from Geneva Medical College (now SUNY Upstate Medical University College of Medicine) in New York in 1849. The first African-American woman to graduate from a medical school in the U.S. was Dr. Rebecca Lee Crumpler who graduated from the New England Female Medical College in Boston in 1846.

Med school today

Today there are 125 MD granting institutions, most of which still follow the curriculum that was proposed by Flexner and all of which require the MCAT. Thing have changed however, most notably the student and medical school faculty body. Each year, a little over 17,000 students start their first year of medical schools, close to 30 percent of whom are minorities. In 2004, 50 percent of the entering class of medical students and 45 percent of the graduating class were women.

--Ivana Nikolic

In 2005, 37,364 people applied to medical schools in the United States, and 17,004 of these people were accepted and enrolled later that year. Of the 46 percent of applicants accepted to medical school, there is no GPA or MCAT score that guarantees acceptance.

Medical schools

There are a total of 125 allopathic American medical schools, with locations in 44 states, the District of Columbia and Puerto Rico. New York State has the most medical schools with 12, followed by California with eight and Illinois and Texas each with seven. On the other end of the spectrum, six states—Alaska, Delaware, Idaho, Maine, Montana and Wyoming—do not have any medical schools, and 19 states have only one medical school. (The admissions scenario is a bit tougher for students from these states, as their in-state options are limited.) Of the 125 medical schools, 75 are public institutions, whereas 50 are private institutions. The difference between the two is that public schools get funding from state governments, whereas private schools rely on tuition, fees and gifts for financial support. Because public schools are state funded, they take mostly students from within their state (which usually comprises 80-90 percent of students), so this gives in-state students a huge advantage in the selection process. Some of these medical schools are quite large and have multiple campuses and over 300 entering students a year, such as the University of Illinois College of Medicine. However, others are quite small and admit roughly 40 students a year, such as Mayo in Minnesota.

Many schools provide students with the opportunity to complete other degrees in combination with their medical education, such as a PhD, law degree, Master's of Public Health or Master's of Business Administration. Another possibility is a MD/PHD program, also know as a Medical Scientist Training Program, or MSTP. This program supports individuals who are interested in pursuing a career as a physician-scientist. We will discuss the MSTP later on in the guide. If you are interested in a particular dual-degree program, it is best to contact schools directly to determine if they offer the programs that interest you.

Price tags

The cost of attending medical school varies greatly, with private schools generally being more expensive than public schools. The average yearly cost for an in-state resident to attend a public medical school, which includes tuition and fees, was $19,961 in 2005-2006, whereas the average yearly cost for an out-of-state resident to attend a public school was $38,865. The average cost for a state resident or non-resident to attend a private medical school was $38,190 and $39,024, respectively (please note that most private schools have the same tuition for both in-state and out-of-state students. However, a small number charge less tuition for in-state residents). Although it can bc informative to look at the average costs of medical schools, it is important to remember that the tuition and fees vary greatly even amongst private or public schools. For instance, the most expensive medical school in the country for non-residents is not a private school, but a public state school, the University of Colorado, which cost non-residents a whopping $75,739 in 2005-2006. The most expensive public medical school for state residents has an annual price tag of less than half of this, which is the University of Minnesota-Twin Cities with a 2005-2006 tuition and fees of $30,998. In contrast, the least expensive public school for state residents was East Carolina-Brody in North Carolina with an annual cost of $9,068, whereas the least expensive public school for non-residents was the University of Puerto Rico at $17,248, with the University of Mississippi a close second at $18,309. Among private schools, Tufts University in Boston was the most expensive for both residents and non-residents, with a cost of $46,063, whereas Baylor was the least expensive, costing Texas state residents $12,607 per year and non-residents $25,707 per year.

Given such striking differences, if the cost of attending medical school is an important factor for you, it is essential to determine the actual cost associated with attending each of the medical schools that you apply to. It may be helpful to even do a little investigative work to determine the amount of financial aid, in the forms or grants, scholarships and loans, that students are awarded at particular schools. While data on the indebtedness of the most recent medical school graduates is not yet available, in 2003, roughly 85 percent of graduates had medical school loan debts. The average debt for public school graduates was $100,000, whereas that for private school graduates was $135,000. It is estimated that these values will continue to rise, and by 2007, the average public medical school graduate will owe roughly $117,000, and the average private medical school graduate will owe roughly $150,000.

The student

There is no particular set of guidelines that gets a person into medical school or makes a person a successful physician. However, it may be helpful to know some basic statistics about the most recent applicants and matriculates. In 2005, there were 37,364 applicants, which was up 4.6 percent from 2004, though not nearly as high as the peak number of applicants of nearly 47,000 in 1996. Of the 37,364 applicants, 49.8 percent were women and 75.7 percent were first-time applicants. California residents accounted for the highest number of applicants, at 4,288, while Rhode Island had the least at 71. 46 percent of the 37,364 applicants matriculated to a medical school in 2005. 49 percent of those were women with an average age of 23, whereas the average age of male matriculates was 24. 63 percent of applicants attended school in their state of residency, whereas 37 percent went out-of-state. The mean MCAT verbal, physical science, biological science and writing scores for 2005 applicants were 8.9, 9.1, 9.5 and P, respectively. As may be expected, the average MCAT verbal, physical science, biological science, and writing scores for accepted students were slightly higher at 9.7, 10.1, 10.4 and P, respectively. Scores range from one to 15 on each section. The mean score is usually around 8, with a standard deviation of 2.5. Thus, a score of 13 on a single section means you have scored higher than about 95 percent of test takers, while a score of 3 means you only scored higher than about 5 percent of test-takers. The average total GPA of applicants was 3.48, with a breakdown of an average science GPA of 3.37 and a non-science GPA of 3.60. For medical school matriculates, the average total GPA was 3.63, with a science GPA of 3.56 and a non-science GPA of 3.70.

Although all of these can numbers can seem daunting, we hope that you can use this basic information as a starting point as you consider how you can best market yourself to be accepted into the medical school that is the best fit for you.

All data is from the American Association of Medical Colleges web site: www.aamc.org

--Sarah Evans

THE SCOOP

The Nuts & Bolts of Applying to Medical School

Chapter 1

The Application Process

The application process begins long before you start filling out your med school applications. You've got to do your homework. Your academic requirements, grades, MCAT scores and interviews will determine where you apply and were you attend medical school.

Undergraduate academic requirements

One of the biggest myths surrounding the medical school application process is that the applicant must be a science major, particularly a biology or chemistry major. In actuality, a medical school applicant may major in any subject area he or she chooses. Regardless of the major one chooses, an applicant only needs to complete medical school admission prerequisites. Prerequisites differ from school to school, but the standard usually consists of eight semester-long classes broken down as follows:

- Two semesters of basic chemistry
- Two semesters of organic chemistry
- Two semesters of biology
- Two semesters of physics

Most medical schools also require one to two semesters of basic college English or writing courses. The good news is that most undergraduate institutions have similar requirements in order to graduate, and fulfilling these requirements will typically also take care of the medical school prerequisite. But be aware that some medical schools will not accept Advance Placement (AP) English credit to satisfy this requirement, and will expect at least another semester of English. Also, some schools require one to two semesters of mathematics, particularly calculus. You should research your schools of interest to find out what prerequisites to complete in order to be considered for admission. This information is usually readily available on the medical school's web site or through your pre-medical advisor.

With only eight to 10 semester classes devoted to the prerequisites required for admission, students can use the rest of their time to major in any subject area they choose. Many students end up choosing biology or chemistry anyway because the common medical school prerequisites coincide with the prerequisites for a biology or chemistry major. Also, many students feel that a strong background in biology or chemistry will help prepare them for the MCAT. But if one examines the data provided by the Association of American Medical Colleges (AAMC) showing the correlation between MCAT score and undergraduate major, there is no evidence indicating a background in biology or chemistry will provide a higher MCAT score (data available at http://www.aamc.org/students/mcat/examineedata/char99.pdf).

If a biology or chemistry major doesn't affect MCAT scores, which major should you choose and why? Well, who better to give advice on this question than successful medical school applicants? In the chapter dedicated to academics, students will give you general academic advice, as well as reasoning behind their choices in majors. While there is a vast array of reasons behind their choices, you will find one unifying theme: pick a major that you will enjoy. Not only do students usually do better in subject areas they enjoy, but college only lasts four years. If you don't enjoy your major for those four years, you'll probably be miserable and regret the decision in the long run.

--Willem Bok

The MCAT

The Medical College Admission Test (MCAT) was designed to assess knowledge of scientific principles and concepts through the use of problem solving, critical thinking and writing. In short, the MCAT tests both aptitude and knowledge. One could think of it as a synthesis of the SAT, which tests aptitude, and the ACT, which tests outside knowledge. First developed in 1928 as a way to decrease attrition rates in medical school, the MCAT has undergone several revisions, the most recent of which was to change the subject material to emphasize the skills and concepts identified by physicians and medical educators as prerequisite for the practice of medicine. The paper form of the test was also converted to a completely computerized format in 2007. The test is developed by the Association of American Medical Colleges (AAMC) in conjunction with its member U.S. medical schools. The MCAT is an unavoidable challenge that must be faced when applying to any medical school. It is one of the critical factors that medical schools use to evaluate an applicant, so it must be taken seriously.

In 2007, the MCAT will be offered on 22 separate testing dates, 20 of which are between April and September, with the other two test dates in January. The test is administered in Thomson Prometric Testing Centers, which are facilities set up throughout the country for the administration of various computer-based standardized exams. It is usually recommended that students take the MCAT about 18 months before they plan to enter medical school though they can take as far in advance as needed and up to three times total without needing special permission. For instance, if you plan on entering medical school in the fall of 2008, you should plan to take the test around April of 2007. The bottom line is that a medical school needs your MCAT scores to evaluate your application and it takes about 30 days for scores to be released after the test date, so plan accordingly.

The only way to register for the MCAT is online at www.aamc.org/mcat. You will be able to register at this web site six months prior to the test date. It is highly recommended that you submit your registration early to ensure that you will be able to take the test at your first choice test center and to avoid any late fees. This will help to alleviate the additional stress of having to travel to an unfamiliar location to take the test. It is important to note that there is absolutely no walk-in registration.

You can take the MCAT up to three times each year, although you must complete an exam before registering to take another. Please note that when your scores are reported to medical schools, all of your previous scores are sent. Therefore, it is best to feel fully prepared before attempting to take the test. Never take the official test for mere practice.

Taking the MCAT is expensive! In 2006, the regular examination fee was $210.00 with a late registration fee of $50.00. There is no indication that these prices will be reduced in the future, so be prepared to pay at least this much at the time you register for the test.

--Michele Blank and Allen Hwang

Where to begin

For most applicants, the formal application process for medical school starts with filling out the AMCAS application, which can be accessed through the Association of American Medical Colleges web site at www.aamc.org. This electronic application is typically known as the "primary" application, and is a common application that goes out to all of the medical schools to which you are applying. Almost every medical school in the country requires you to send them this initial application so that they can screen applicants for their individual or "secondary" applications. The primary AMCAS application requires that you fill out personal information, record grades for your classes, describe extracurricular activities and write a personal statement. You must also send them an official copy of your transcript. Along with your primary application, AMCAS will also send your MCAT scores to medical schools. Secondary applications are sent by individual schools after they screen your primary application. These often require you to write several additional essays and fill out more personal information, but this is highly dependent on the school, so you should be prepared for the extra time commitment and pay close attention to the unique deadlines for these supplemental applications.

Please note that there are a few schools that do not require AMCAS, and you must apply to these schools directly. Most of these schools take part in the Texas Medical and Dental Schools Application Service, including the University of Texas Southwestern, Texas A&M University and Texas Tech University. Further information about this process can be found at www.utsystem.edu/tmdsas/HomepageMS&Pre-HlthAdv.htm.

There are several key points to consider when deciding what schools to apply to. No matter the credentials you possess, you should apply to at least one school where your chances for admittance are higher than at most other schools, often called a "safety." The chance of getting into your state school is often better than your chances for getting into a private school because your state schools are required to accept more applicants from your state. Typically, 80-90 percent of a state school's student body consists of in-state residents. It is always wise to apply to your state schools, even if you prefer not to go there now; you may change your mind if that is the only school you are accepted to. However, just because the odds are in your favor at state schools, do not think that admission is guaranteed at any medical school. The disclaimer here is that even so-called "perfect" applicants get rejected from medical schools, so be aware that the process is imperfect and thus can be unfair to even the most deserving candidates.

It is always a good idea to apply as early as possible. Some schools have a rolling admissions process in which they send out acceptances throughout the interview season, and as the number of acceptances goes up, it gets more competitive for the late interviewees. There is also an early decision program in which certain medical schools participate. This program requires that you apply to only one participating school, which requires filling out the AMCAS by August 1, and waiting to hear back. If accepted, you will know by October 1, and you must attend this medical school. You can only apply to other medical schools once you have been rejected from you early decision school or received an official release from them allowing you to apply elsewhere. Check with individual schools to see if they participate in this program.

There is no magic number of schools to apply to, but the majority of students send their AMCAS application to between 10 and 30 different schools. If you get more interviews than you care to attend, you can always withdraw your application from individual programs, so it is better to apply to a lot of medical schools and get plenty of interviews, rather than apply to a few schools and get a small number of interviews. With that said, it is important to realize that AMCAS charges an application fee of $160 for one medical school designation, and then charges an additional $30 for each additional medical school. Individual schools often charge an additional fee for their secondary applications, most of them around $50, so be aware of this additional cost of applying.

See Chapter 6 for additional advice on the application process, writing essays, getting recommendation letters, and dealing with the stress of it all.

--*Vik Devisetty*

The medical school interview

If you've made it this far and have received an invitation to interview: congratulations! Breathe a sigh of relief! This means that the selection committee has reviewed your application and believes that you have the potential to succeed in medical school ... at least that is how you appear on paper. The medical school interview is an opportunity for both the interviewer and the applicant to see if they are the "best fit" for one another. Both you and the institution have marketed yourselves in attempts to appeal to your respective desirable audiences. What better way to determine if the accolades and reputations are rightfully deserved than to meet in person? Consider this your time to impress, and to be impressed.

There is no set formula for how many interviews a medical school will offer during a given application season. Most institutions will provide you with this information, or at least have it available through the admissions office. For example, Harvard Medical School released their most recent class statistics online, reporting that, out of over 5,000 applications, just under 800 interviews were offered to fill 165 available spots in the entering class of August 2005, boasting a *U.S. News*-reported acceptance rate of 5.2 percent. In addition, there are medical schools that preferentially give interviews to applicants who are in-state residents. Be sure to do your research before you spend money submitting secondary applications to institutions to whom you are geographically unattractive.

In preparation for your interviews, recognize that each institution will have a unique interview day format that has likely existed and worked well for them for several years, with only minor changes along the way. So, while a typical interview day may involve an early morning arrival followed by greetings from the admission officers, a financial aid presentation, lunch with current medical students and some version of a tour through the facilities, there are certainly variations on this theme. Your interviews could be in the morning or in the afternoon. You may have to interview with three other applicants all at once in a panel format. On the contrary, you could be subjected to a series of three or more one-on-one sessions that last less than 15 minutes each. The interviewer could be a current medical student, an attending physician, or a faculty member that has retired from practice. The key is to having an edge up on this process is to do your research. This can't be stressed enough. Visit web sites. Ask upperclassmen who have already gone through the process. Read medical school guidebooks that thoroughly profile each institution and their interview day. The hints on what awaits you on interview day at a particular program are all available and there should be no surprises. You'll be ready for the ethical debate, the "stress-test" of the window that just won't open, and the doctor who is notorious for asking applicants about the steps of the Kreb's cycle. You will do yourself a huge favor by knowing what to expect ahead of time.

Finally, the general rules to interviewing well are by no means rocket science. Rather, they are common sense principles that, for whatever reason, are easily shaken from our minds once we are put in the "hot seat." A key component to interview success is to know the institution, be able to communicate what it has to offer you and, most important, what you can add to the entering class. This is also the perfect chance for you to get all of your burning questions about the medical school answered. When asked, "do you have any questions for me?" ask some! Show that you're interested and that you have seriously considered their institution as the best place to obtain your medical education. And last, but not least, be cordial and courteous to everyone you meet, including the other applicants.

--Erica Taylor

Financing Your Medical Education

The cost of a medical school education is no small number, and that number is growing. In 2005, the average debts for medical school graduates were approximately $138,000 for private and $110,000 for public school students. Needless to say, financial assistance for medical school may play an important role in where you decide to go. Aside from any savings you or your parents contribute, financial aid, grants and scholarships will likely fund your medical education.

Financial aid

When going through the financial aid process, it is important to remember that each school may have different requirements and deadlines when it comes to the necessary forms. However, the first step for the majority of schools is to fill out the Free Application for Federal Student Aid (FAFSA). You can fill out the form online at www.fafsa.ed.gov. At this site, you will find all of the information you need to complete the FAFSA form. The point of FAFSA is to figure out the financial status of you and your family. In addition, most medical schools use information from the FAFSA form to determine the amount of private loans and grants for which you may be eligible. Schools will often require additional forms for calculated financial aid. It is important to talk with the financial aid departments at each school to determine what you need to do. More than likely, once you are accepted, the financial aid department will send you information on their specific requirements. The medical school web sites are also good resources.

The FAFSA form is available after January 1st of the year in which you plan on entering school. Fill out this form as early as possible. Although the deadline for filling out this form for federal aid is usually in late June, most medical schools require this form much earlier (typically around March). Again, talk with your potential schools regarding this due date. It is not necessary for your parents to have filed their tax returns before filling out this form, but it does make the process easier.

After you have filled out the FAFSA form, completed other forms required by individual schools and been accepted by some medical schools, your work is done for the most part. You should make schools aware of sudden financial changes you may have experienced. Once you have been accepted and filled out the proper financial aid materials required by the schools financial aid offices, the school should make you aware of the money for which you qualify. With this information, you can then make a decision as to which school is best for you.

Be diligent about researching the loans you plan to receive. Different loans have different payback schedules and differences in interest rates. For example, many schools participate in the Federal Student Loan Program. Through this, you may be eligible for subsidized loans, which means that the federal government pays the interest your loan accumulates while you're still in school. Only once you are out of school does the interest start accumulating. Most other loans start adding interest the minute you take out the loan, which makes subsidized loans a great way to avoid excess debt.

Scholarships and grants

Of course, the best form of financial help is the kind you do not have to pay back. There are many sources out there for scholarship money. It is your job to go out and find them. Your best resource may be the schools to which you are applying, so do not be afraid to ask what they offer. There are also many programs targeted towards underrepresented minorities and the economically disadvantaged. A list of possible places to begin your search appears in the Appendix of this book. Some schools do not publicly advertise their scholarships, but you are automatically considered after you apply and are accepted. Finally, many schools offer grants based on your financial status. This differs from scholarships in that it is not merit-based. It is similar to scholarships in that you do not need to repay them, unlike financial aid, which you do need to repay.

The application process itself is a very expensive one. The financial aid chapter will discuss specific programs designed to help the economically disadvantaged cope with this issue. The rest of the chapter will illustrate how three students tackled the issue of financing their medical education and how financial aid affected their decision.

--Sujay Kansagra

Undergraduate Academics: Choosing a Major

CHAPTER 2

Pre-Med Myths

During my sophomore year at Stanford, about the time that I had resolved to apply to medical school, I came upon an open letter written by a physician to premedical students about "Pre-Med Myths." The letter debunked many of my misconceptions about the pre-medical process and emphasized that there is no single best path to medical school. Among those myths was the notion—prevalent among my pre-med peers—that there was a relatively fixed curriculum, handed down through the years, which made you look the "best" to medical schools. Few of the classes in that artificial curriculum (most of which were large lectures with professors jaded by years of teaching premeds), held any allure for me, so after reading this enlightening letter I resolved that as I prepared for medical school, I would not do so at the expense of my academic interests or happiness. I still majored in biology because I enjoyed the material, but I did not follow the standard track, and I made sure to take the classes that most appealed to me. The following are suggestions about choosing classes drawn from my own undergraduate experience.

Avoid taking burdensome classes JUST to make your transcript look stronger

It's very difficult for medical schools to appreciate the rigor of an applicant's course load, but it's very easy for them to appreciate your grades and GPA. Admissions committees notice when a transcript is obviously short on science classes and they recognize to some degree that some majors are more demanding (such as engineering). However, for the typical applicant (a science major) who lies between these extremes, the difficulty level of a student's course load is rarely clear. As a pre-med I realized that it would be silly to take, say, the advanced math series or an especially heavy course load JUST so it would "look better" on my med school application—no one could tell the difference. However, if the extra burden caused my grades to slip, that surely would be noticed. That isn't to say I didn't take a lot of difficult classes, but they were all ones in which I was genuinely interested (i.e., I didn't take them for the sole purpose of making my transcript courses seem difficult), and as a result, I did very well in them. I also didn't hesitate to carry a heavy course load, indeed I often took the maximum permitted credits, but if necessary, I took the extra classes pass/fail to keep my schedule manageable.

Requirements for your major may be more flexible than you expect

While I really enjoyed the subject of biology, the department's standard curriculum involved many classes in which I wasn't interested. Furthermore, there were a lot of non-biology courses that I wanted to take in my brief four years of undergrad. Fortunately, by writing some respectfully convincing petitions, I was able to create a course of study that satisfied both my major and me. The department required a number of core/distribution classes, which tended to be large lectures filled with pre-meds, but the department was happy to let me substitute some of these more onerous classes with upper-level classes, which were smaller and more engaging. Like many pre-meds, I had done a good bit of summer research, so I asked to have it count in place of one of my required biology lab classes. Similarly, I skipped the dreaded but (supposedly) required first intro chemistry lab, took the more interesting second lab, and then petitioned to have the requirement for the first lab waived. Lastly, I found biologically relevant electives that really excited me in other departments (such as anatomy and biomedical informatics) and asked that they count toward my major. The end result was that I took only the biology classes in which I was specifically interested and simultaneously freed up time for non-biology classes. When I applied to medical school, I had a strong, well-rounded transcript as well as the satisfaction of getting the most out of my undergraduate years.

Consider taking some classes pass/fail or dropping a class if you are overwhelmed

If you are already carrying what your school considers a "typical" course load, and there is another class you'd like to take but you are concerned you will have trouble excelling in all of them, consider taking the additional class pass/fail. What constitutes a "typical" course load varies between schools, but keep in mind that the goal isn't to make the standard pre-med curriculum easier. I would not suggest this if you tend to carry a light load nor would I recommend using this as a way to slide through many of your med school requirements. The idea is that concern about your GPA shouldn't preclude you from exploring other academic interests. At Stanford, students were expected to take an average of 15 units per quarter, and when I exceeded this level, I often took the additional classes pass/fail. In this way, I was comfortably able to take classes like Advanced Italian and American Health Policy during otherwise full semesters. On the other hand, if you've registered for several classes and you realize that you've taken on more than you can handle, consider dropping a class. You're probably better off dropping one class and doing WELL in the others than doing poorly in all of them. Remember, on your application the GPA is glaringly obvious, while the dropped class is nestled among the other classes in your transcript. Certainly, you don't want to make a habit of dropping classes, but a single dropped class is more easily overlooked than an entire term of questionable grades.

The United States is one of the few places where students must complete an undergraduate degree before beginning medical school. Unfortunately, many students become so preoccupied with the pre-medical process that they fail to take full advantage of this opportunity for personal and intellectual development. Certainly, the pre-medical coursework is significant and there are some requirements that cannot be avoided, but be very skeptical of pre-med "common knowledge" and those who suggest that there is a BEST pre-med curriculum. If there is a class you are dreading but feel you must take because every other pre-med takes it, talk to a pre-med advisor or check the various requirements and make sure it is truly necessary. I have written here specifically about courses, but I found that the same principles hold true for volunteer work, taking time off, extracurricular activities and research. Preparing for medical school is certainly a lot of work, but with thoughtful planning, you need not sacrifice your other interests or your peace of mind.

--Gabriel Howles-Banerji

The Science Major

The discussion on choosing a major is divided into two fronts: those who believe majoring in science would appear more prestigious on applications, and those who believe one should choose a major based on interest only. Just about all admissions' offices will tell applicants that a major doesn't matter as much as whether the applicant is a strong student. Although most incoming first-year medical students tend to come more from a science background, it is often just a matter of self-selection. Medical school applicants are more likely to be interested in the basic sciences, and wish to learn more about them as undergrads. I ended up deciding on a science major, and thus, will discuss what I believe are the advantages of this track, as well as discuss my personal experience on deciding on my major.

The advantages of a science major

The medical school curriculum is almost entirely science-based, and modern medicine is heavily rooted in basic science topics such as physics, biology, chemistry and math. More in-depth exposure to one of those topics as an undergrad will make learning about how that topic applies to medicine easier in med school. These basic science classes also teach you a way of thinking and studying skills that will be important for medical school. This is because basic science puts more of the emphasis on memorization of concepts and information followed by application, which is much of what medical school entails. Having majored in science makes fulfilling your pre-medical requirements easier, as the typical biology or chemistry major will cover most, if not all, the prerequisite courses while a student who majors in the fine arts may need to take additional courses before applying. One additional advantage of choosing a science major is taking classes that cover the materials in the MCAT more in depth. Much of the overlap provides better understanding of the fundamentals, which serves as review in itself.

Which science major should I choose?

Most admissions offices seem to believe that what is important is whether the student was at the top of his/her class, regardless of the class itself. So, should one choose an easy major just to have a higher GPA? Certainly having majored in quantum physics should appear more impressive than floral design (a major I once seriously considered at the University of Florida). Again, the decision comes down to interest. Pick a field in science that interests you the most. Most colleges will allow the student to be undeclared in major selection until the second or third year; taking introductory classes early in the first two years will allow you to make a more informed decision in major selection. Also check out the graduation requirements for the different majors and talk to the advisors and upperclassmen.

I once overheard a newly matriculated freshman exclaim, "I really want to be a doctor, but I hate chemistry!" Even if you suspect you will strongly dislike a course, give it a try first. Science classes in college are extremely different from the science classes in high school, and the focus is shifted more from repetitive busy work to comprehension and application. When it comes down to course selection, talk to as many people as possible, because having the right/wrong professor can make all the difference. Often times my favorite classes in college were not in topics that I had a particular interest for, but classes that had phenomenal professors.

Certainly getting into medical school has been compared to jumping over hurdles, with excelling in the required courses and doing well on the MCAT being two large ones. Although taking more challenging courses may appear more impressive to the admissions committee, only doing mediocre in them really isn't impressive. Think twice before signing up for a course that you are not interested in.

Real life: Being a science major

I majored in biochemistry in undergrad, and in retrospect, I feel I landed in the right major solely by luck. In high school, I found biology to be an interesting memorization list, and I excelled in chemistry based mostly on intuition. One thing that I did know for sure was that I wanted to be a doctor. Based on that sole conviction, I selected a major that would "help" me get into medical school, or at least make medical school easier for me down the road. I chose biochemistry because the number of required classes for graduation was much less than the typical biology tract, and the tract was more flexible, allowing me to take more non-science classes. Only well into my major did I realize how much I loved molecular genetics and learning about the workings of the body on a cellular level. From that point on, I took a graduate level biochemistry course and completed my senior research project on gene activation. Having a flexible major allowed me to learn more in depth about biochemistry, and still gave me the time to learn how to arrange floral centerpieces.

--Hui Xue

Engineering

Years of calculus equations, physics labs and endless problem sets—at first glance, these exercises may seem irrelevant for medical school. Why even consider engineering if ultimately you want study medicine?

First and foremost, the sole purpose of undergrad studies doesn't need to be preparation for medical school. These schools accept people from all academic backgrounds, and, in fact, most med schools try to build a class with diverse experiences. As a clinical physician, you may not need many of the technical skills acquired through engineering, but your problem-solving background could be invaluable in analytically approaching medical diagnoses and academic research questions. Consequently, if you have a love for engineering, go for it. But also keep in mind some of the lessons I've learned along the way.

First, although med schools might view you as unique with an engineering background, in most cases they will NOT be impressed by what is probably a more difficult course load than the standard pre-med track. Regardless of the difficulty of your classes, you need to excel in your coursework to have a shot at the top schools like Harvard, Johns Hopkins and Duke. When I was an undergrad at Stanford, rumors were rampant that med schools added GPA points for those with difficult majors; from what I know now, this is completely untrue. If you have received poor grades in your first few engineering classes, it is time to seriously reassess your study habits or even consider another major if you are certain you want to be a doctor. The reality is that GPA is a crucial factor in determining your medical school acceptance. I, for instance, did not focus enough on the books during my first two years, and my grades were not up to par for medical school. Once I saw fellow Stanford students with similar GPAs being rejected from medical school, I realized the importance of GPA and I began working harder to improve my grades dramatically. So the lesson is don't lose hope if you feel like you've underachieved thus far in your academic career, but you ultimately need to do well if you're hoping to get into a medical school.

Next, if you love engineering (or whatever major you're in) make sure you gain enough experience in both medical and engineering environments to convince yourself that medicine is your optimal career path. If you're an engineering major, it is clear you have some quantitative, analytical tendencies that probably won't be emphasized in clinical medicine. Shadow doctors and work with patients to gain a feeling for the day-to-day life of a practicing clinician. For the opposite perspective, you might consider interning at an engineering company. Such experiences solidified my career goals.

Third, both for you and for the application process, obtain a variety of health service experiences. As an engineering student, it is difficult to take the breadth of courses that medical schools expect. Volunteer experiences, even if only for a few hours a month, will clarify your sincere interest in the medical field, and are especially helpful during the interview when some interviewers will expect the stereotypical analytical and dehumanized engineer.

A difficult adjustment from engineering's conceptual nature is the reality of medical school academics. There may be little conceptual thinking and limited intellectual exercises—often rote memorization of pathways, medications and chemical structures. Personally, this transition has been smoother simply because I entered medical school expecting this change. Know that although the initial academic portion can be painful, the rewards are reaped later as you develop clinical skills that allow you to develop broad differential diagnoses for a variety of patient presentations, and to then trim this list of diagnoses down to the most likely few through logical reasoning.

Finally, most medical schools favor humanistic applicants. With engineering's time constraints and restricted academic choices, it can be difficult to portray yourself as the caring individual you really are. Do something significant with your extracurricular activities to demonstrate these qualities. But for anyone, including a future doctor, who loves science and abstract thinking, engineering is a great academic track.

--Robi Goswami

What if I Don't Want to Be a Science Major?

I can remember agonizing for weeks, if not months, before I had to make my decision during the spring of my sophomore year. One thing that made it easier on me was that during that time at Princeton, all the departments held open houses for students deciding on majors. At these open houses, we were able to speak to other students, discuss possible options with department faculty, and were given an outline on the types of classes and projects that were expected to be fulfilled in order to satisfy graduation requirements. I eventually settled on majoring in psychology.

You may already know what you want to major in during college. But take a step back and try and entertain the possibility of a different one you haven't been set on since freshman year (or grammar school as the case may be). I think this advice is particularly important for pre-med students who believe that it is absolutely necessary for them to be science majors (with the majority choosing to concentrate in biology). Yours truly and countless others out there have gained acceptances into multiple medical schools without a science concentration.

I can remember personally in the weeks just prior to when I had to declare my concentration, I was still juggling between three possible majors. What made me eventually narrow it down to psychology was a series of departmental open houses I visited, and advice from family, friends, upperclassmen, pre-med advisors and a personal list I wrote out that contained the pros and cons of each major. Since Princeton not only required a thesis for graduation but also one to two junior papers, I knew that the major I eventually chose would have to be interesting enough for me to stay focused. In addition, I knew that I had to weigh each department's faculty, their ongoing research and their level of involvement in undergraduate advising, since these would be the people who I would work most closely with during the final two years of college. Even if a thesis is not required for graduation, it may be needed for honors or you may choose to write one (and/or undertake heavy research with a professor), in which case choosing a department with a good faculty and track record becomes absolutely imperative.

One of the reasons why I personally decided to not major in a science was the fact that I knew once I started medical school, I would learn all the science that I ever desired (and then some). Essentially, I saw college as my last opportunity to study a subject that I would not have the opportunity to study again and as a chance to help broaden my perspective. When else would one have so much opportunity to spend a term abroad or explore other non-science interests?

--Harold Agbahiwe

Another non-science major

Coming to college, I felt my four years would be a time to explore. As a result, I majored in international relations and took few science courses. I completed my pre-med requirements in a post-baccalaureate program after college. Even though I currently have little practical use for my major, I don't regret my decision. Studying international relations provided a broader learning experience and helped me realize my academic strengths and weaknesses, something I wouldn't have known from high school alone. In addition, I cultivated many important skills, such as writing, critical thinking and viewing the world from a wider perspective. I also had a chance to take a variety of courses I was simply interested in—economics, political science, sociology, art, math and comparative literature. I don't think my major and non-science experience hindered me at all in the med school application process. For me, high school provided a limited scope academically and college was an important time to figure out what I truly wanted to pursue. My only regret was that I didn't know earlier that I would apply to medical school. Had I known, I probably would have tailored my major more to my career by studying international health.

Despite my major, however, I did make sure I studied the basic pre-med requirements thoroughly, such as introductory biology, general chemistry, organic chemistry and physics. I also focused on doing well on the MCAT to reflect my proficiency in the sciences, which I believed was particularly important since I was a non-science major. I chose to do the minimum science requirements so that I could use the extra time to travel, do some research and also save money. I also felt I would be studying those subjects again in medical school anyway. In retrospect, medical school courses are much more quickly paced and, at times, I do question whether it would have been a wiser choice to obtain a stronger science background. But so far, I've been pretty happy with my decision.

Some of you may not have completed the basic pre-med requirements and may take a post-baccalaureate program afterwards. When I was choosing a post-baccalaureate program, I often wondered whether the name of the school was important and whether I needed to do an established program, such as the Harvard or Johns Hopkins programs, or if I could just take pre-med courses at any school. I ended up taking the pre-med requirements at my state school, the College of Charleston in South Carolina, which did not have an established post-baccalaureate program. Throughout the application process, I didn't feel the name of the school was crucial as long as I had done well in the pre-med courses and also on the MCAT. (The name of the school may have some weight in particular cases, such as if one is applying to the program's medical school or is interested in getting recommendations from professors at a well-known university.) But state school programs are generally cheaper and they often use the same textbooks as private universities. I felt that my state school prepared me well for the MCAT. The school maintained a high quality of teaching, granted me access to the professors, and allowed ample opportunities to do research.

Before I applied to medical school, I also thought very thoroughly as to why I wanted to do this, and toward that end tried to gain as much experience as possible in the healthcare field. I wanted clear reasons in my mind as to why I specifically wanted to be a doctor after several years of studying social sciences. I believed that it was important for me to enter a profession that I found academically challenging and emotionally fulfilling, and I wanted to make sure I made the right choice. Doing volunteer work in a rehabilitation center and also tutoring a biology course confirmed my belief that I wanted to work with patients and that I really enjoyed teaching. Alongside my major, these were great activities to keep my experience diverse and interesting.

My approach to the undergraduate years and applying to medical school was simply to work hard, study what interested me, make sure that I showed competency in the pre-medical sciences and really question if medicine was truly my calling. It is an approach that worked well for me.

--Emily Choi

Doubling Up

Sometimes the whole is larger than the sum of its parts, and after I thought about it, I realized that by doubling up majors I gained something in my undergraduate experience to which neither pure science nor pure humanities majors have access. Namely, studying both gave me the opportunity to compare and judge vastly different approaches to the accumulation of knowledge. In time, I was able to decide for myself the relative merits of each approach and then find a balance in using them in my life.

To provide a little background, I entered college as a biology/biochemistry/bio-whatever major like many other aspiring medical students. After one semester, I knew that this was not how I wanted to spend the rest of my college days. My problem with biology had nothing to do with a lack of interest in the material. I found most of it very compelling, but I felt that much of the work of undergraduate biology involved rote memorization of chemical equations, anatomic diagrams, and taxonomic charts. Students' main tasks were to report what past scientific luminaries had already accomplished. The results were undoubtedly beautiful, but there was something deeply unsatisfying about merely describing other people's work.

I turned to physics to provide me with more concrete problem-solving and along the way, I picked up some philosophy classes for variety. Both kept my attention, and so majoring in both fields was a natural transition. My experience was that physics and philosophy attended to entirely different, but equally thirsty, parts of my curiosity about the world. While the first gave me practice in applying cold logic and steely rationality to the analysis of the concrete world, the other kept me abreast of the messy ways we try to capture some truth about another world, one of abstract thoughts, feelings and concepts. During my studies, I found that some scientists were rather disdainful of what they felt was the humanities' self-serving soft research, and likewise, there were philosophy professors who found the scientists' work to be antiseptic, soulless and, worst of all, meaningless. As it happened, they were both wrong about the other: science and the humanities are equally enriching and studying either alone limits one's view of the human experience. They are simply different ways of looking at the world and as a doctor, I imagine that there will be times when scientific level-headedness is called for and other times when humanitarian sensibilities are more appropriate. If nothing else, preparation in both a science and non-science major has given me a wider selection of tools with which to tackle the challenges of being an effective and compassionate doctor.

--Shervin Shirvani

I entered Dartmouth College wanting to be a physics major. This ended promptly when I signed up for honors physics and realized that I, unlike the other kids in the class, had not been to nerd camp when I was 12 to learn multivariable calculus. Although I managed to struggle through the term, this class was a nightmare for me.

I was vaguely interested in medicine when I came to college, so I decided to take general chemistry. This went well and prompted me to continue taking chemistry classes. During my sophomore year, I took an organic chemistry sequence of classes designed for people going into chemistry. I loved it, and my teacher was phenomenal. Also, I decided that as long as I was doing okay in these classes, I would continue with chemistry.

However, I was also taking the required pre-med biology classes and was becoming more and more interested in the biological applications of chemistry. I opted out of biology because I was not willing to memorize enough material to do well in those classes and decided that I would become a biophysical chemistry major. This was a chemistry tract that focused on the chemistry of proteins, a topic that fascinated me.

My freshman year, I took a required freshman seminar called Eco's Echoes, taught by a professor of medieval history. I was fascinated by history, and decided to take another history course with him that spring. My sophomore year I took a course on the history of the Revolutionary War. Although I loved the professor, I struggled with the class. At one point, when I was writing my 20-page term paper, he told me, "Jim, you shouldn't be a history major because you don't understand time." Although I was discouraged by this, I decided to pursue the history major in addition to chemistry.

My schedule was hectic; my majors took up 28 of my 35 classes at Dartmouth. Ultimately, I decided that I would stick with the two majors as long as I was enjoying the material. This is how I ended up with two majors.

I loved being a double major because it allowed me to totally switch gears when I got sick of one subject. Also, it was probably a significant advantage when applying to medical school simply because it is unique. There are not too many history and biophysical chemistry majors applying to medical school. However, this is not a reason to be a double major.

I firmly believe that you should study what you are most interested in and that if you do this, you will both do better in your classes and be a happier, more well-rounded person. For me, studying history and chemistry allowed me to enjoy a breadth of curriculum that I will never have access to again. One problem with medicine is that it is very narrowing. The demanding medical school curriculum does not usually allow time for one to pursue outside academic interests.

There are also some very significant disadvantages to being a double major, most of which I did not realize when I started down this path. First of all, you need to make sure that you love the material you are studying because you will not have time to take other classes just for pure interest. Second, you may not be able to explore one of the majors as fully as you would have if you were focusing only on one subject. Finally, you will have a very difficult schedule. I spent the fall of my junior year working on my chemistry thesis and then went to Rome to study history for the rest of the year. This meant that I had to take seven chemistry classes my senior year (not exactly a slack senior schedule, especially when you throw medical school interviews into the equation).

A double major has some significant rewards, both in terms of the material it will allow you to master and also in the sense that you have a much broader framework from which to approach medicine. However, it comes at a significant cost. Keep this in mind when deciding if this path is right for you.

--James Hotling

Changing Your Major

I was good in science, enjoyed design, liked calculus and liked learning how things worked. At North Carolina State University, a university known for its science and technology programs, I chose electrical engineering without a second thought. But two years and a power company internship later, I knew it wasn't what I wanted to do with the rest of my life. I took a nutrition course and an anatomy class and began to realize I liked the life sciences much better than what I considered the dead sciences of circuits and programming. But what was I supposed to do? I had 80 hours of electrical engineering credit and half of a minor in economics. I decided I wanted a career somewhere in the healthcare field but wasn't sure where. I was looking into everything from PhD to physical therapy to MD programs.

But before I could think about that, I had to decide on an undergraduate major. I looked into biomedical engineering but barely any of my course work transferred, and it would be at least three years until graduation. Faced with spending a considerable amount of time in graduate school, I thought four years was plenty to spend getting my undergraduate degree. Also, to get into those graduate programs, there were significant prerequisite courses. Despite these challenges, I was reluctant to completely give up on electrical engineering. Although it wasn't what I wanted to do, I was doing well in the program and it was a very versatile degree. It seemed a waste to throw it all away, and of course no one likes to quit. So after much consternation, I decided to finish my EE degree and add a second major in biochemistry. This would fulfill all the required coursework for professional school in the health sciences and, if I didn't get in, I could get a job with my EE background. It would require one summer full of organic chemistry and about 21 hours for the last four semesters, including finishing my economics minor.

Well, it only took one semester for me to realize I was insane. A very smart advisor gave me some much valued advice which I now offer to you: he said a BS degree is a BS degree and they were pretty much all BS, so there was no need for me to have double BS, I should just pick the BS I liked and run with it. Sure enough, I finished my biochemistry degree and my economics minor in four years. I had plenty of time to prepare for the MCAT and more time to devote to my extracurricular leadership projects, not to mention time to travel, see friends and go to football games.

Looking back, the moral of my experience is to do what you like and like what you do. I try not to think of my engineering coursework as wasted, but a valuable step in learning about myself. As it turns out, I had a great time in college, and many great advisors helped me along the way. Don't be afraid to turn to them when difficult decisions come up. Chances are, they have seen it before and will have valuable insight. All you have to do is ask.

--Andrea Havens

Research

CHAPTER 3

In modern medicine, biological research is intimately tied to the practice of clinical medicine. At academic medical centers, many clinicians are involved in basic, transitional or clinical research, often times devoting most of their careers to this work. Even for those doctors that choose not to be directly involved in doing research, the medical profession requires at least some rudimentary knowledge of research techniques if a physician is to understand primary journal articles that provide the most up-to-date information—a necessity given the constantly expanding and evolving nature of medical knowledge.

Given this emphasis on research in the medical field, a number of pre-medical students choose to do research in preparation for medical school. However, the necessity of doing such work, whether science or non-science, is debatable. With the exception of MD/PhD candidates, research experience is not a definite requirement for a successful medical school application.

Questions Every Wannabe Researcher Should Ask

If you decide that you want to do research, the question most students ask is "where do I start?" The first research position is often the hardest to get, since you have no lab experience to offer a mentor. With a little determination and effort, though, finding that first lab will not be too difficult as long as you begin with the right questions.

When should I do research?

First, you should decide when you want to do research, either during the academic school year or during the summer. Both times have their advantages and disadvantages.

If you choose to do research during the school year, you will have less time to focus on your experiments, since you will be splitting your time between classes and your lab. Depending on your class schedule, you could easily end up running to your lab in between classes or late at night to finish an experiment! On the other hand, if you are not sure how much you are going to enjoy doing research, doing research during the school year means that you probably will not be expected to be in lab all day long for the majority of the week; working in the lab part-time is a way to ease into doing research rather than having it take over your life.

The other option is to do research during the summer, usually through some type of internship. This option offers you more time to focus on your project and a more continuous laboratory experience. Most likely, summer research will be a full-time job, so you have to decide whether you want to be in the lab for that much time each week. Also, since you are working with a limited time frame, you will have less flexibility in terms of the length of the stay in your lab. More often than not, summer research interns do not get the chance to follow their projects to their completion or publish papers.

What type of research should I do?

The answer to this question should be whatever you are interested in! Initially, you will need to decide whether you want to do non-science research (e.g., public health), clinical research, basic science research or translational research. Clinical research is patient-oriented research that often involves direct interaction with patients. In contrast, basic science research is bench research not involving human subjects, which can encompass a range of modalities—ranging from genetics research to cell or tissue research, to animal studies, to computer modeling. Translational research is considered a bridge between basic and clinical research with the goal of taking information obtained through basic science research and applying it directly to answer a clinical question.

You also should try to narrow down a research area to what appeals to you the most.

Where should I do research?

The two main opportunities for pre-medical students to do research are with a faculty member of your undergraduate institution or at an outside research facility through an internship.

For the first-time researcher, finding a faculty member as a mentor offers the most flexibility. At most universities, faculty members are approachable and open to having students work with them (let's face it, you're free labor!). Since you can contact more than one person while looking for a mentor, you will have a greater range of labs from which to choose. Educator-researchers often make better mentors, since they are accustomed to working with students. Being familiar with the typical student's lifestyle, a faculty member might be more understanding when you cannot come into lab because you have those three papers and two exams coming up. If you decide that you want to do research during the school year, working with somebody on campus probably will be your only choice unless you live within commuting distance of a major research facility.

Research positions at outside research institutions, such as the National Institute of Health, tend to be more competitive, often involving lengthy applications. You might have to wait months to hear back about the status of your application and will have no guarantee that you will get a position. Also, given the competitive nature of most internships, you usually do not get to choose what lab you are in—the mentors usually pick which students they want. A variety of types of internships exist; some are paid while others are unpaid. Internships are available during the school year while others are specifically for the summer months. Once in the program, your hours and the expectations of your performance will be less flexible than if you were working with a faculty member at your university. On the other hand, these positions are competitive for a reason. They often offer extra perks, such as lecture series, trips to conferences, etc. The lab facilities tend to be topnotch, and you will get to interact with leading scientists.

Finding an outside research position

The first thing that you want to do is gather a list of places to which you might apply. Look on the Web; a simple web search on "research internship" will link you to multitudes of resources. One great web site is www.science.gov/internships/ which offers a listing of internships with government institutions, sorted by the required level of education. There also are internship databases available on the Web, such as monstertrak.com. Talk to people at your school's career services. The opportunities are out there if you look for them. Most importantly, though, make sure that you get this information EARLY in the year, i.e., in the fall if you are applying for a summer internship. Many of the bigger, more competitive (and usually the most worthwhile) internships, such as the National Institutes of Health, have early deadlines! Once you have identified a list of places, fill out applications and more applications—something you will become very familiar with as a pre-med!

Finding a lab at your university

There are a couple of different ways to identify some faculty members whose labs interest you. First, you can talk to your course instructors for any related class to see if they have any suggestions about faculty members with research interests that parallel yours. The director of undergraduate studies (DUS) for whatever area you are interested in (e.g., the biology DUS) might be willing to offer some guidance as well. If all else fails, there is always the Internet. Most academic centers have a faculty research directory online. Search through the database, and try to identify faculty doing research that you might find interesting.

Often times, universities will have class credit for research, and they will have a list of faculty that are willing to have undergraduate students in their labs. This is a great place to start if your school has such an offering.

Once you have a list of people in mind, start contacting them. E-mail is a quick, painless way to make initial contact; ask whether the faculty member has time to meet with you and discuss his/her research. Not everybody will get back to you, and not everybody will have spaces open in their labs. Chances are, though, that if you e-mail a fair number of people, you are bound to get a couple of responses. From there, set up meetings with some faculty members, and get a feel for their labs.

What type of materials do I need before contacting people?

The requirements will vary—some faculty members will not ask for anything at all while an application for a place like NIH will require almost as much paperwork as your AMCAS! Here are some useful web sites to get started on your hunt:

National Institutes of Health: www.training.nih.gov/student/index.asp
National Science Foundation: www.nsf.gov
FirstGov for Science: www.science.gov/internships (for lots and lots of internships)

In order to not be caught off-guard, though, you might want to put together a curriculum vitae and cover letter as well as get a copy of your transcript. Getting some recommendations from science professors would be in your best interest, too.

Even more things to consider when choosing a lab

Each lab is different. Make sure that you check out the facilities, hours and compensation, as well the personnel and project.

Your mentor

How accessible is your mentor? How much independence are you going to be given? Do you want to have control over the experiments and given free reign to decide the direction of the project or would you rather be led through the process by your mentor? What type of atmosphere does your mentor encourage—a relaxed lab or a very serious one? Talk to the other members of the lab! Smaller labs may have as few as two or three people, while large labs may be 50 or more. These people might be able to give a more accurate assessment of the type of conditions you might be facing. Then, decide which type of environment suites you best for instance, some students prefer constant guidance while others flourish under minimal supervision.

Lab facilities

How much lab space will you have? How many other students are there in the lab? Lab space might not seem that important when you are looking for a lab initially but when you come into the lab bright and early on a Saturday morning to run an experiment, only to find that there is no bench space, it quickly becomes an issue. Usually, if the mentor is offering to take you on, chances are there is enough space, but better safe than sorry. Finally, what type of facilities do you have access to?

Hours

What type of hours are you expected to put in? (weekends, mornings, etc.) Will your mentor be flexible if you need to take a day off?

The project

How interested are you in this type of research? What types of experiments are involved? Will you have to do animal work?

Compensation

Outside research positions often come with some type of stipend. If you are working with a faculty member, though, you may or may not (usually not) be paid for your time. Many undergraduate institutions offer class credit for doing research, which is particularly common at large universities.

--Melissa Chung

The Science Track

To be completely honest, I first decided to get involved in basic science research because I thought it would be a useful thing to write on my medical school applications. However, looking back on my experience, that is the least of what I gained. During my two years of research, I learned many laboratory skills, which allow me to now better understand the research of others. I also learned about scientific writing and how to create poster presentations (which are very similar to high school science fairs, but with a more professional display of your work) and write scientific papers for publication. Most importantly, I ended up becoming extremely interested in my work. Here is the story of how I got started and how I benefited from the experience.

During my sophomore year of college at Rutgers, I started to search for a lab at my university in which I could work over the summer. I knew that I would be taking my MCATs in August and a Princeton Review course at night. I decided that if I worked in a laboratory during the day, I would be able to have a flexible schedule and more time for studying than if I worked a conventional nine-to-five job.

I had noticed previously that there was an alcohol studies laboratory at my university that was looking for highly motivated students to fill a summer position doing research in neuropharmacology and behavioral studies. I called and made an appointment for an interview with the lab's principal investigator (PI) and then printed out a complete transcript and resume to bring with me. I did a PubMed search on the PI before the interview and had skimmed over several of her recent articles before I arrived. This background research allowed me to see if I was interested in the research being conducted in the lab and to impress upon my interviewer my knowledge of her work in the field of animals' endocrinologic motivation in alcohol drinking behavior.

I worked at the alcohol studies lab for independent research credit that summer and continued to work there during my junior year. I learned data processing and animal testing skills while I was there and quickly developed a routine that felt quite comfortable. However, I was not given the opportunity to develop my own project and spent most of my time carrying out the tasks my advisor instructed me to perform. After a year of working there, I grew tired of this pattern and knew there was no more for me to gain from that laboratory. I decided to start looking for a new one.

I asked my friends in the sciences to see if anyone knew of a laboratory that might be taking students. One of my friends was working in a neurotoxicology laboratory with a prominent principal investigator who ran a very large and well-funded laboratory. My previous laboratory experience within alcohol studies helped me in obtaining a position at this laboratory. After meeting with the PI, we decided that I would work there over the summer for pay, and then continue during my senior year for credit and write a senior thesis. This situation turned out to be ideal. The neurotoxicology lab offered many more opportunities than the original lab that I had been with. While there, I learned about cell culture, various forms of microscopy, neuroscience and toxicology. I also was able to present my work at a national conference, was awarded research fellowships and merit awards for my work, and was published in a well-known toxicology journal.

I discussed my senior research project at every one of my medical school interviews. It allowed my interviewers to see that I was excited about my research and gave me something to discuss that made me unique from their other interviewees. Many of my interviewers conducted research themselves and were happy to see that I was so interested in and knowledgeable about my own project.

Based on my experiences, I would give the following advice to college students considering basic science research. First, find a lab that interests you and that has had recent publications. Second, choose a lab where you will be able to work on your own project and not merely perform experiments for other people. Then work towards the goals of being able to present your work at a conference or publish it in a journal. If you find that you have reached a point where there is nothing more you can gain from the lab you are in or you no longer enjoy it, consider looking for a new lab where you will be able to gain novel skills and be exposed to different fields of study. Finally, I would suggest that you only get involved in basic science research if it is something that you enjoy and can get excited about. If you find that you do not enjoy it, there are many other interesting things you can do with your time such as community outreach programs, leadership roles at your school, tutoring, working as a teacher's assistant (TA) and volunteering in the medical field that medical schools will be equally impressed by.

--Rachel Grisham

The Other Side of Research

"Research" is a very different thing in a scientific lab than it is in other fields of study. Studying ancient documents, interviewing subjects for a population survey or providing rigorous mathematical analysis is a far cry from performing microsurgery on rats or growing tissue cultures. To your chagrin if you are a non-science type, medical school admissions personnel are well aware of the difference. Moreover, most medical schools give a lot of credit to students who have participated in significant scientific research.

So why do non-science research at all? Frankly, do it if it's your thing. You can't spend your whole life and college career trying to impress medical schools, and it is well worth pursuing your other interests now. You may not have another opportunity to do art history research, or, if you want to do that on the side after medical school, the experience during college will be invaluable to you as a person, even if not as a med school applicant. Besides, most medical schools are turning over every stone to find "diversity" these days, and why not show yours with some solid economic development work or research into the history of quilting in North America?

If you want to go down this road, however, there are a few things to consider. First, many medical schools really do not look at non-science research as on par with research in the traditional scientific fields. Even if your other credentials are outstanding, you should expect to lose points from certain schools on the basis of your lack of scientific research experience. I was personally told by an admissions committee member at a prominent research-oriented school that not having done scientific research counted against me in their "scoring" of my application.

So what should you do about it?

Perform some scientific research in addition to your more beloved pursuits. It really would be a good experience, and it will help you get into medical school. If you don't take this approach, you'll be more likely to find interviewers asking about your science deficiency than being interested in your non-science prowess. For example, I was interviewed by a PhD in physics, but never by a PhD in archaeology. He was my only interviewer that day and questioned me incessantly about the basic science I had not pursued. I think if I had done a little bit of scientific research to allay his fears that I was scientifically incompetent, then he may have been more interested in what qualities I did possess, and I might have gained admission to the school.

If you can't bring yourself to obey piece of advice number one, then be sure everything else in your application is solid.

Show a strong commitment to medicine by gaining plenty of clinical experience and attain superb grades in the science courses that you take (and it wouldn't hurt taking a few extra).

Look for ways to make some of your research medically relevant, even if not from the scientific side.

While pursuing a graduate degree in applied economics, I wrote a theoretical paper on the role of vaccinations in the cost analysis of infectious diseases. In addition, my thesis work utilized worldwide epidemiological data to make its arguments. Thus, even if you are not willing to sit at a lab bench during your discretionary time, there are ways to show your ability to contribute to "academic medicine."

There's a difference between experimental psychology research and ancient history. In certain social sciences it will be much easier for you to argue that at least the general method used is similar to science: constructing hypotheses, designing repeatable experiments and obtaining results. If you spend most of your time in the humanities, you may want to consider some science work on the side.

Science and non-science work at various levels?

Science gets people into med school. But what if the non-science work is well-published, or graduate-level, or if the researcher spent time at a prestigious institute or center? Make sure to spell these sorts of things out on your application. Your neighborhood medical school admissions committee does not know the top journal in your field from your school newspaper, so if you have done something exceptional, make sure they know it, both by stating it on your application and by obtaining a reference from a professor who will tell them.

My final piece of advice is to look at what you are doing every semester or two and think, "What will this do for my chances of being admitted to medical school?" I thought that if I excelled in all of my chosen activities, as long as I completed the literal prerequisites for medical school, I would have no problem getting in. The fact is that your favorite medical school may have a category labeled "scientific research" in which you can get from 0 to 10 points. If you did none, and nothing that could even be construed as scientifically relevant, you are now working on a 90-point rather than a 100-point scale. No, you probably won't be able to find out anyone's "scoring" system, at least not until you've been rejected and call back to ask why. But you have two defenses. First, you can be sure to do at least some small project in every relevant category (science research, clinical medicine, volunteering and so on). Second, you can carefully select your schools of interest by shying away from those who present themselves primarily as a research-based institution.

--Jeremy Wingard

Clinical Research: Bridging the Gap

Like half of my entering undergraduate class at Stanford University, I had already decided on pursuing a career in medicine. I had already spent time during high school shadowing physicians, volunteering at hospitals and conducting basic science research for a medical institution. From prior experience, I knew that I enjoyed the in-depth investigation of interesting topics that research afforded me. So, continuing to research seemed to be the inevitable conclusion.

Early in my freshman year, I had become interested in cultural psychology and had begun working as a research assistant in a cultural psychology laboratory at Stanford. Fortunately for me, Stanford also offered a competitively awarded scholarship program designed to encourage independent research among undergraduates in social sciences. At Stanford, these are not that common, as about 25-35 are awarded per year only to sophomores after a competitive grant application review process. This scholarship allowed me to combine my interests and design a research project to explore the social aspects of depression for women in India. The opportunity to conduct research on my own was an invaluable addition to my undergraduate experience. I chose to pursue clinical research initially because it was a convenient merger of my interests in medicine and social sciences.

Independent research can be a truly liberating experience as well as intellectually stimulating. I enjoyed engaging faculty discussions as well as reading background literature. I literally began from scratch, just lightly perusing the psychiatric literature until I became more focused on investigating major depressive disorder. My personal facility with Indian languages and my familiarity with the Indian culture were deciding factors in further focusing my project on India in particular. Throughout the project, bridging the social sciences and the medical fields were difficult because of the multitude of diverse lines of research converging about depression. At times, assimilating all the different theories and recommendations from different faculty advisors was arduous. The research process, from the assimilation of background literature and completing the application for funding, to gaining faculty advisors and writing of my thesis, was time-consuming, and at times, obsessive. But these very struggles and learning experiences gave me a sense of being an active participant in research, rather than a passive assistant.

Conducting research in India turned out to be a completely different affair than clinical research in the United States. Not only are there differences in expectations of doctors and researchers, but the entire cultural milieu is different. Looking back on my experience, it feels surreal to have been trying to conduct a thorough study interviewing patients with depression in rooms with paper-thin walls not quite reaching the ceiling. I encountered plenty of challenges, both dealing with research design and with research ethics. Immersion in a world with vastly different cultural expectations and regulations enhanced my awareness of the tacit provisions of scientific research. I believe that my experience in India gave me a deeper insight into not only research but the practice of medicine in other cultures.

In hindsight I would have liked to have guided experience in a clinical setting before attempting to carry out independent research. Guided research is useful for exploration of different areas of research as well as for the experience about the research process that can be gleaned from professionals. This type of opportunity can provide insights into the process of research, from grant writing and funding to independent review boards.

On another note, research can also strengthen a medical school applicant's background by adding unique experiences and insights. Most elite medical schools seek a diverse class of individuals, with different experiences to enhance the experiences of one's peers. Clinical research not only demonstrates a zest for academic learning but also diversifies a student's interests. Moreover, since clinical research involves patient interactions, the research provides insights into another facet of patient experiences. My medical applications and interviews were heavily peppered with anecdotes and insights stemming from my research experience, which were distinctive and concise vehicles that could convey the diversity of my medical experiences as well as linger in the minds of others.

--Sarita Patil

No Research? No Worries!

While a lot of my friends were off curing cancer, playing with rats, cleaning test tubes, making photocopies or just surfing the Net at the numerous research labs scattered across campus, I spent my free time taking non-science courses, playing basketball in the gym, or simply relaxing and enjoying the company of friends and family.

A lot of people feel it is necessary these days to do big-level research to get into the medical school of his/her dreams. Let me first start off by saying that doing research of any kind will generally help you out as an applicant, but it is not necessary in and of itself to get you into medical school. Better said, it is not necessary at all if you spend your time doing another equally productive or enlightening endeavor.

The main reason why I opted not to do research was simple: I hated working in labs on projects that were uninteresting to me. Some may say that I could have found a lab where they were doing something up my alley, but I don't particularly like doing basic science research of any kind. That is why I was usually studying business or at the gym instead of grinding away at the lab bench.

I always have had a passion for medicine, but medicine is such a broad field and encompasses many facets of education (e.g., book learning, hands-on experience, basic science research, etc.), that there can be some aspects of medicine one may not love. I didn't like research. I also thought that I might have wanted to go into private practice and felt that my energies might be better spent pursuing other interests that I both liked and that might also be of service to me out in rural America or wherever I decide to set up shop. For me, this other interest was business, and for some of you, it may be art, foreign language, travel, etc.

One of the things I was able to pursue in lieu of doing an extended research project was travel abroad. That was an excellent experience and gave me some great insights into life and invaluable experiences that I would have never been able to get in a lab. While I realize the virtue and importance of lab work for many, for some of you out there, including people like myself, research may not be the best thing to do. If this is the case for you, you may want to look into other areas where you can not only enhance your medical school application, but where you can also learn some life lessons and gain some knowledge.

Of course, some will try to convince you that there are medical schools that may not even give your application a second look if you haven't already discovered the secret to spinal cord regeneration or the mechanisms that mediate Viagra's effects. This is wholly untrue, and in fact, the top tier medical schools are more likely to see diverse pursuits as an asset. You will have plenty of time in medical school and afterwards to do gel-electrophoresis and mice experiments.

In general, while you should definitely take into account what can and will help you for a future career in medicine; it needn't necessarily be in the field of science. Many of the greatest physicians were artists, writers, explorers, etc. You also should do something you love, because chances are, if you love it, you will excel in it—and if you excel in it, it could very well be your entrance into the medical school of your choice.

--Nabeel Hamoui

Extracurriculars

CHAPTER 4

It is no secret that most medical schools find extracurriculars, especially community service, an essential part of every application. Most schools devote a large percentage of their secondary applications and interview time to discussing extracurricular activities and what you have learned from these experiences. Unfortunately, medical school admissions committees must make difficult decisions on who to interview based solely on the student's application without ever speaking with the applicant. If you do not get an interview, you will not have any way of showing a school who you really are. Most schools do not even provide sufficient time during the interview process to really get to know someone, since the typical interview only lasts 30 minutes. Therefore, the community service and extracurricular activities in which you participate say a lot about you and your dedication to the field of medicine.

There seem to be two schools of thought when it comes to extracurricular activities and community service. One viewpoint is that students should choose a few organizations or projects that are especially important to them and maintain their involvement over a long period of time. Commitment allows students to build relationships with those they help and absorb a great deal from their experiences. Meanwhile, the other viewpoint is that a student can gain a wide variety of experience by participating in many smaller projects. This approach provides exposure to different people and circumstances, but lacks the continuity and commitment some schools are looking for. To help you decide which method is best, we'll start off getting advice from students that have chosen different paths when dealing with extracurriculars.

All extracurriculars should be mentioned (if there is room) in your application. On most applications you only have a specific amount of space to discuss extracurricular activities, so choose the ones that best demonstrate your personality and dedication to the medical profession. Be sure to mention how the experience has affected your life or you as a person. You could do some rare and extremely powerful work, but if you do not mention how it has affected you, the admissions committee may overlook it. By the same token, if your project is small but you get much out of it, an admissions committee may find this appealing.

This chapter concludes with a look at traveling abroad and summer opportunities. The more cultures a person experiences, the easier it is to understand, appreciate and navigate differences between his or her thoughts and feelings and those of the patient. As this country's population becomes increasingly diverse, being able to consider unfamiliar point of views will become essential for effective patient care. Also, there are actually many summer programs for students contemplating entering the medical profession. These are usually held at medical schools and may cost some money, depending on the program. Check out www.aamc.org/members/great/summerlinks.htm for examples of some programs offered. The summer programs introduce the students to many aspects of medicine and medical education which can assist them in deciding whether or not medicine is what they want to practice, as well as give those that are sure a head start in the field. Also, many undergraduate institutions will have either formal or informal opportunities to meet with medical students to ask them questions about the application process and what life is like as a medical student. If your school doesn't have this, suggest it to your pre-medical advisor or pre-medical student club. Or, if there is not a medical school associated with your undergraduate institution, call a school that does and ask when these session take place.

--Nathan Mall

A Question of Quality

As a medical school applicant, I was a little different. Many medical school applicants have a large number of extracurricular activities that span a wide range of interests. When I applied to medical school, there were only four extracurricular activities listed on my application and three of these activities focused around one central interest: sports. While I did not have a large number of extracurricular activities or a wide range of interests, my extracurricular activities still stood out on an application since at least one was a quality extracurricular; in other words, an activity that is extremely time consuming and requires a great amount of discipline and dedication.

For two thirds of my university career, I was a varsity swimmer at the University of North Carolina. A typical week required around 20 hours of training: three 90-minute morning practices a week, six two-hour afternoon practices, and three one-hour weight lifting sessions. Swimming is also a year-round sport. Most swimmers are only out of the water for one month a year (two weeks in the spring and two at the end of summer).

At the end of my freshman year, I decided to attempt a B.S. in Business Administration in addition to the B.S. in Biology I had already begun. This meant that I had to take classes during both summer sessions for the remainder of my undergraduate years (I hoped to be done in four years). 12 hours of classes and swimming made my summers pretty busy. Since I attended a large public institution, I would often avoid dealing with the hassle of an appointment with the pre-med adviser, thinking I could learn what I needed to know from books or online sources. For example, I knew that a pre-med student should try to gain significant clinical and/or research experience outside the classroom, but I figured that medical school admissions offices would understand that between swimming and my double major, I didn't have much time for anything else. Unfortunately, I was wrong.

During the middle of my junior year, after finally meeting with the pre-med adviser and talking to several doctors familiar with the admissions process, I realized that it was important that I obtain some clinical and/or research experience. I found several opportunities, but all required a year-long—commitment. These new opportunities added another activity to a summer that was already full (in addition to swimming and classes, I was planning to dedicate some major time to study for the MCAT). With the upcoming summer in mind, I had a discussion with my swim coach, and we both agreed I should stop swimming in order to have more time over the summer and the following year. By summer, I had stopped swimming, was volunteering in a local E.R. eight hours a week, and I started club water polo so I could stay active in the water. I also started coaching at a local YMCA at the end of the summer after the MCAT. These are the other three extracurricular activities that I listed on my application to medical school (combined, these probably took up more of my time than swimming).

I began interviewing in October of my senior year, and I quickly saw a trend emerge with regards to my interviewers' questions. At about half of the schools I interviewed, my interviewers were extremely impressed with the amount of discipline and dedication I had put into swimming. At the other half, I usually heard questions similar to "You've never shadowed a doctor?" "How come you didn't spend time in a hospital before the end of your junior year?" or "You're a biology major, are you not interested in research at all?" Well, it was no surprise that when April came around and acceptances went out, I was accepted or waitlisted upper tier at the first half of schools I mentioned, and rejected or waitlisted lower tier at the latter group of schools. Also, I called some of the schools that had rejected me or those that had not granted me an interview to find out the reason. Those that decided to tell me all mentioned a lack of clinical and/or research experience. Even though I had been in a hospital setting for several months, these schools evidently thought my clinical experience had come too late and was not enough or was of the wrong type.

So what's my advice? First, I recommend a quality extracurricular activity or one that takes a good bit of your time, because it shows admissions officers that you have a good amount of discipline and dedication. But remember that whatever extracurricular activity you choose, you are planning on becoming a doctor. So I would either choose an extracurricular activity related to becoming a doctor (clinical or research oriented), or if not related to the health field, you should do something in addition that is related to the health field. And make sure you enjoy whatever it is, especially if it is medically related. If you don't enjoy your health-related extracurricular, try another before you quit on medicine altogether. If you have a few bad experiences, you may be in the wrong career path. You're only in college four or five years. Make the best of your time!

--*Willem Bok*

Just Do It

The best thing you can do is find a service commitment to your community and get out there and just do it. As a freshman at UNC-Chapel Hill, I applied for a position on the Freshman Focus Council, which was Carolina's interpretation of a freshman student government, because I wanted to meet more people. I joined Ebony Readers Onyx Theatre because I loved acting in theatre settings. I became active in the Black Student Movement because I wanted to unify with fellow students of color for a common cause. I joined the Carolina Athletic Association because I wanted tickets to basketball games. By the time I had graduated, I had taken leadership positions in all of these organizations and a few others.

Interestingly, of all of my activities, not a single one was medically related. Yes, I want to be a physician. Yes, I wanted to attend medical school. Yes, I was a loyal pre-med. However, my involvement was not driven by my desire to get into medical school but by things that interested me. For some of you, your interests will lie solely in medically-related issues. However if it does not, it's okay!

My involvement has taught me so much more than I could learn in a book or from a lecture. My involvement and leadership activities have given me basic tools that I can build on. In my junior year, I decided to run for student body president. After finally committing to the grueling student election race, I rarely slept, practiced speeches constantly and hounded voters with buttons, talks, etc. I improved my public speaking abilities and learned how to let my guard down and to trust others. Ultimately, I did not win, and I expected myself to be devastated. However, I was not. I pulled myself together, made phone calls to thank my workers, and went about my daily life. Most importantly, though, I did not quit. I decided to take an officer position within my student government to continue to push my initiatives.

My experiences have prepared me to fail, to succeed, and most importantly to try again. As future physicians, the hardest part for us to realize is that we will not cure everybody, we will not heal everybody, we will not prevent people from dying, and at times we will not get the outcome we had hoped for. Though it seems like such a simple issue, it will take us years to truly hold on to that thought.

--Dustyn Baker

Variety: The Spice of Life

Here's a fairly typical idea of what my college life consisted of for four years. My days were taken up with classes. My afternoons and nights belonged to the cacophonous fury of those things we like to call "extracurricular activities." For four years I balanced such things as: guiding tours, photography, yoga classes, working as a waitress, sorority life, volunteering as an usher at the local theater, swimming, salsa, working as a camp counselor and being an undergraduate researcher with a full course load.

During college, I learned what I needed for a career in science through my classes, but I learned what I know about life and people from my extracurricular activities. Through my various endeavors, I became part of different communities, activities and ways of life I never would have seen if I had focused solely on my pre-med curriculum. As a science tutor for a high school outreach program, I caught the bus three days a week into the heart of Oakland's ghetto and saw children living in conditions I thought only existed in the Third World. By working at the UCSF melanoma clinic, I witnessed people locked in a battle for life against their own bodies. Through dance, I tried to prove that white girls really can have rhythm. Hopefully one of these days, someone will actually believe me.

The wide range of my extracurricular activities exposed me to both uplifting and difficult experiences. Attempting improvisational acting helped me keep a healthy dose of humbled reality. Watching a patient that I had come to love pass away shook my foundations and left me up late at night. But each experience blessed me with another piece of knowledge that helped me to slowly piece together a more complete view of the world.

Given Berkeley's thriving, zealous pre-med population, I heard much speculation during my undergraduate years about what medical schools wanted to see in terms of extracurricular activities. My advice would be to do only those activities in which you have a genuine interest. Hunkering down for four years and working in a lab that causes you only misery or spending time de-worming orphans when you would much rather be watching Oprah probably won't fool the admissions committees. Don't waste your time, or the time of the people who will be interviewing you, expounding upon how something changed your life when it didn't. Admissions committees hate liars.

I think the extracurricular activities offered around most college campuses are some of the greatest opportunities I have come across in my 23 years. The best thing about college is that nothing is permanent. Although you eventually should try to show a certain level of commitment to those activities that interest you, you are free to explore as many options as your heart desires. If you have thought about banking, you can try an internship. Cooking? Sign up for a class and bring on the spatula. Medicine? (Hey, you're reading the book, aren't you?) Volunteer at a clinic or hospital.

--Christiane Haeffele

Summertime

For traditional applicants who have always attended school, summer is that one season when a focused commitment to another activity is possible. With my summers, I wanted to try new things and get deeply involved in projects that I thought would be fun and rewarding. I never worried about what medical schools would think of my summer activities and I still believe that as long as you get involved with a project, activity or class that you are really interested in and give it serious commitment, medical schools will appreciate that. I was fortunate to find interesting jobs and classes that allowed me to try new things and teach me things that were useful in the application process, medical school and in life outside of medicine. I hope that you get a similar sense for the diversity of opportunities out there.

After my freshman year as an undergraduate at Duke, I never even considered the possibility of going anywhere for the summer other than back home. Through a program sponsored by Children's Hospital Medical Center in Cincinnati, I had shadowed pediatric surgeons the previous summer. Those hours of shadowing had been the transformative experience when I realized that medicine was what I wanted to do with my life. However, I also wanted to find out what medical research was like. So I e-mailed one of the pediatric surgeons with whom I had kept in touch and proposed my idea. I wanted to work on clinical research projects so that I would get time to see more patients and have more time in the operating room. She was very receptive to the idea and even found funding so that I was paid for my time. In the morning I would work on research projects requiring lots of retrospective chart reviews, mostly of liver transplant patients, and in the afternoons I would attend rounds and surgery. It was a great way to spend a summer and still be at home with my family. Keeping in touch with the people you have met and worked with in the past and showing a lot of interest in their field is sure to help when it comes to finding great summer opportunities like this one.

My chemistry major required a lot of cell biology and biochemistry courses (my degree emphasized biochemistry), but none of those classes had a lab, and I needed two biology labs for medical school. Wanting to both do something different with my next summer as well as get lab credits, I decided to study at the Duke University Marine Laboratory in Beaufort, North Carolina, a picturesque small town on the Atlantic coast. It was a great place to study biology and the environment in a small class setting with engaging faculty and beautiful scenery. Other educational programs exist in marine biology across the country, but Duke's program is one of the largest and most education-oriented. It is open to all students, not just those from Duke, and the friends I made there came from all over the world. Many schools are members of the Marine Sciences Education Consortium and have pre-approved the courses offered there. I attended both summer sessions that summer, each one lasting five weeks. I also pursued independent reading and research in the Marine/Freshwater Biomedical Center there at the Marine Lab. Many students, including myself, consider their experiences at the Duke Marine Lab to be the highlight of their undergraduate educational experience. Furthermore, because of the small student to faculty ratios at the Marine Lab, students really get to know their professors, and many go on to ask their professors for letters of recommendation for medical and graduate school. I would recommend that everyone seek out similar opportunities where they can work in small class settings with dedicated professors on exciting topics. Often your college advisor, director of undergraduate studies and favorite professors can give some suggestions about where to look.

Summer is the one time of the year when you can give a project 100 percent commitment. Dedication to activities is something that medical schools look for when evaluating applicants. It is better to do a few things really well than a lot of things poorly. For this reason, I focused my last summer on biochemistry and pharmacology research at Duke. Duke had funding available that could pay me a salary while I worked in the lab. To get funding, I recommend starting the search months ahead. One good source is to approach your university's office of research, the director of undergraduate studies in that department or your advisor. I found that there is a lot of funding available for student research projects. Looking on the Internet is one way, but if your mentor knows of internal or discipline-specific sources of funding, those are usually better, more hassle-free and easier to get. Many professional organizations provide funding for undergraduate summer research in their area. Find out what organizations your mentor belongs to and consider looking there. For example, the American Heart Association has awards available for undergraduate research in cardiovascular research. Working in the lab, although a more common experience for pre-meds than the activities of my other two summers, was a great experience because it complemented my coursework in biochemistry and allowed me to practice many of the techniques that I had read about.

When you look for summer activities, I would encourage you to be open minded about the things you might consider doing. Medical schools will appreciate unique and creative activities to which you have shown a serious commitment.

--David Evans

Opportunities for Minorities and Economically Disadvantaged Students

I am a strong proponent of using each summer in college for learning, exploration and furthering one's career goals through research, internships, or summer programs. In January or February of each school year, I visited my school's Career Planning and Placement Center (most campuses have one and I think this is the best place to start) and met with a counselor to learn more about opportunities for the upcoming summer that matched my interests. Successful pre-med upperclassmen were also an invaluable resource for finding out about opportunities. I chose summer experiences with the following goals in mind:

- Provided funding since I was a poor college student
- Provided insight into potential career paths since I also wanted to learn more about other fields related to medicine
- Facilitated hands-on learning to increase my skill-set
- Focused on underserved, disadvantaged communities since this is the community I ultimately hoped to work with
- Provided diverse locations so I could experience living in different parts of the country

I spent my summers after each year of college in the following ways based on these criteria:

Freshman year

- I did a one-month health policy internship for my U.S. Senator in Washington, D.C. to explore whether I wanted to pursue a career in this field.
- I interned at the United Nations Sub-Commission on Human Rights meeting in Geneva, Switzerland for one month to have an experience living outside of the country and learning more about human rights.

Sophomore year

- I earned an Undergraduate Research Opportunity grant through my school to research alternative healing methods used by the Gullah people of the South Carolina Sea Islands for one month.
- I attended the Summer Medical and Dental Education Program (SMDEP) at Case Western Reserve University in Cleveland, Ohio for six weeks.

Junior year

- I did a violence prevention internship at the Centers for Disease Control and Prevention in Atlanta, Georgia to further explore careers in public health for three months.
- I believe dedicating at least one summer to pursuing a program specifically designed for pre-medical students is invaluable. It is a great way to learn more about getting into medical school and introduces you to a wide network of pre-med students from other schools, many of whom will be your future colleagues. A good place to begin looking for these programs is on the American Association of Medical Colleges enrichment programs web site at http://services.aamc.org/summerprograms or www.aamc.org/students/minorities/. I also suggest talking to your pre-med counselor. I'll share my experience at one such program as a representative example of how these experiences can positively contribute to your education.

SMDEP

I learned about Summer Medical and Dental Education Program (SMDEP) from my pre-med counselor at Stanford during the winter of my sophomore year. SMDEP is a six-week summer program that was originally designed to help students from minority groups that are underrepresented in U.S. medicine (African Americans, Latinos and Native Americans) gain admission to medical school. The program has been expanded to include economically disadvantaged students and students with an interest in working with underserved communities. 12 medical schools across the country host this program to help students with MCAT preparation and the medical school admissions process. SMDEP is free and includes full tuition, housing and meals.

I used my pre-med counselor's advice, the SMDEP web site and testimonials from SMDEP alumni to choose the three sites to which I would apply. The application was due in March and I learned in April that I was accepted. I chose to attend Case Western Reserve University's SMDEP program in my home state of Ohio. All of the basic information about SMDEP is available on their web site (www.smdep.org/) so I'll share the more personal side of the experience, including how I decided to attend SMDEP, the student perspective on the program and how SMDEP personally benefited me.

At the point I attended SMDEP, as a sophomore, I was questioning whether I wanted to continue the grueling pre-med track. I was tired, frustrated and unsure of what to expect in medical school or as a practicing physician. I hoped that spending a summer immersing myself in medical school preparation would help me make a more educated decision about what I wanted to do with my life.

A typical day at SMDEP consisted of waking up for breakfast around 7 a.m. and attending classes from 8 a.m. until 12 noon. After lunch, each day was a little different. Everyone was in small groups for a writing and communication course; however, on alternating days, we could choose between study tracks on MCAT preparation or study skills. Evenings were dedicated to studying, special outings, speaker series, programs or homework.

The 8 a.m.-noon curriculum was dedicated to pre-med courses taught by Case Western faculty. This time was helpful in reinforcing concepts I already knew while introducing subjects I would see the next year; however, there were times of boredom and confusion because it was difficult to gear the classes to everyone's needs since freshman-seniors were in the same class. I strongly recommend researching the curriculums at summer programs of interest to determine whether they are geared for beginning students or students who are ready to take the MCAT in order to choose the best possible fit. The courses were graded and Case Western kept these in our files; however, the coursework did not transfer back to our home institutions.

During the afternoons, we broke out into smaller writing/communication classes that were lead by graduate or medical students. We wrote our personal statements, had them edited and practiced public speaking. They videotaped our speeches and awards were given for the best speeches during the closing ceremony. Since I was at the beginning of the pre-med curriculum at the point I attended SMDEP, I chose the study skills track. Case Western has a full-time person dedicated to helping medical students with learning styles. Many of the invaluable lessons during this class I continue to use in medical school, such as note-taking skills for science classes and effective ways to read scientific textbooks.

My roommate took the MCAT course through SMDEP, which was taught by Kaplan. This was a huge benefit since the course usually costs over $1,000. In addition, people taking the MCAT had built-in faculty members and medical students to help them write their essays and do mock interview with them as they applied to medical school. However, the drawback to this arrangement was that my roommate could not totally devote herself to studying because she was taking classes and participating in activities for the program. If you plan to take the MCAT the August after you participate in a summer program, I strongly recommend going to a program that is specifically geared toward MCAT preparation.

We also had sessions on preparing for the medical school interview and each SMDEP participant had a mock-interview with the medical director of the program. We dressed up and it felt real for the people who were willing to play along and imagine how they would feel during their first medical school interview. One of the most rewarding aspects of SMDEP was the shadowing days. Each student had at least three opportunities to shadow physicians. In addition to getting a better sense of what a physician does during a typical day, I gained a mentor because I am still in touch with one of my SMDEP preceptors.

Without a doubt, the richest resource of SMDEP is the people. The staff and faculty were helpful and continued to support me four years later by serving as a sounding board as I made the decision on which medical school to attend. The medical students were always around and became friends and mentors. They told me things to look for during the application process that I would have never thought of on my own. I made lifelong friends from schools around the country, many of whom were already in medical school when I applied. They gave me great advice on the admissions process and served as housing hosts as I flew all over the country for my medical school interviews. Traveling for medical school interviews is very expensive so having friends in the cities where you interview is a huge cost-saver.

SMDEP was an excellent experience and I went back to college the following fall with renewed resolve to tackle my school's pre-med curriculum. I only highlighted SMDEP because that was my experience, but I encourage you to use your classmates, pre-med counselors and the American Association of Medical Colleges web site to find the best program for you. Strategically think about how you want to spend your summers so you will go back to college each fall with new knowledge and life experiences that will equip you for the future. As my time in medical school comes to a close and I reflect on all of the experiences that brought me to this point, I'm grateful for the people, knowledge and encouragement that I gained by participating in a summer medical education program. I realize that participation in this program marked the pivotal point that firmly set me on the road to becoming a physician by equipping me with the tools, knowledge and people that would help me along the journey.

SMDEP programs sites:

- Case Western Reserve University Schools of Medicine and Dental Medicine
- Columbia University College of Physicians and Surgeons and College of Dental Medicine
- David Geffen School of Medicine at UCLA and UCLA School of Dentistry
- Duke University School of Medicine
- Howard University Colleges of Arts and Sciences, Dentistry and Medicine
- The University of Texas Dental Branch and Medical School at Houston
- UMDNJ-New Jersey Medical and New Jersey Dental Schools
- University of Louisville Schools of Medicine and Dentistry
- University of Nebraska Medical Center, Colleges of Medicine and Dentistry
- University of Virginia School of Medicine
- University of Washington Schools of Medicine and Dentistry
- Yale University School of Medicine

--Ebony Boyce

Going Abroad

I decided I wanted to spend a semester abroad before I even set foot in my first college class. The romance of living in another country, becoming immersed in the culture, learning about my heritage and, of course, traveling around Europe held immense appeal. It quickly became part of my "grand plan," which turned out to be extraordinarily unplanned. I did not realize until the end of my first year of school that the experience would require some sort of academic merit to justify its existence; it was not until my second year that I really began to consider how this experience might contribute to the process of applying to medical school. In hindsight, it played a role in every aspect of the application process, including academic preparation, MCAT and application timing, essay questions and interview conversations.

One major consideration was academic preparation. There were two main factors I had to take into account. The most important issue in my case was careful scheduling of the required courses for medical school. In essence, studying abroad removes one semester from the junior-year schedule, which is when many students either take the second semester of a year-long required course or complete the final requirements for their application. It was necessary for me to carefully plan when I would complete courses such as physics and biochemistry. I began this planning during my second year, but would encourage earlier planning if possible. The second issue was the education I would receive abroad. I spent several months researching the different opportunities and courses offered by each of the colleges in Ireland, the country I had chosen. My final decision rested as much on the opportunity to further my minor in anthropology as the cultural opportunities offered by the National University of Ireland in Galway. I think that the good balance between these two aspects created an extremely satisfying experience.

The second major impact that studying abroad had on my application to medical school was on the timing of the entire process. I chose to travel abroad during the second semester of my junior year, when most pre-medical students take the MCAT. This choice left me with two options: (1) fly back to the United States; (2) find a site abroad to take the exam; or (3) delay taking the exam. I did not plan to study for the MCAT abroad because I did not want to lose any bit of the unique cultural and academic experience. Therefore, I chose not to take the exam that semester because I thought my performance would be diminished by travel to the test site and lack of preparation. I was then left with a decision to sit for the MCAT in August or delay my application to medical school by one year. I chose to take a year off so that I would not be completing my application late in the process, but this is a very individual decision.

The study abroad experience was incorporated into all of my medical school applications in some way and discussed in every interview. Although it did not eclipse any of my other activities, it somehow became a focus of many questions. The semester served as an example of characteristics and knowledge I had obtained during college. Many essays on secondary applications could be answered using illustrations from the semester. As an example, questions about cultural experiences and ability to relate to different types of people were easily addressed with my experience abroad. Interview conversations could often be approached in the same way. For instance, a question regarding characteristics that would make me a good physician could be answered by describing the flexibility and ease in meeting new people that I developed while living abroad. Most interviewers also directly asked questions about my experience, giving me an opportunity to distinguish myself and express some individuality.

Looking back, I realize that studying abroad was an exceptional experience. Although extra planning and thought were necessary to schedule the required courses and to complete the application process, the advantages of spending a semester away were easily worth the effort. I had the chance to become immersed in another culture, meet new people, travel and study new topics. I learned more about the country my great-grandparents had come from and I completed a minor in archaeology with my archaeology of Ireland courses. I will have lifelong memories of learning in the European system, making good friends with diverse backgrounds, walking the streets of Galway, and truly being independent in a foreign city. As an added benefit, I was also able to draw from these unique experiences to set myself apart from thousands of other applicants.

--Molly Boyce

Be Unique

Thousands of applications, everyone wants to help people, everyone has good grades, good MCAT scores…who would you choose? I would choose the ones that stand out from the rest, the ones that are unique. I truly believe this is why I was chosen from the multitudes of electronic applications, personal statements and letters of recommendation.

A friend of my family, who is a physician, recommended that I choose one or two service projects and continue them for a length of time that would allow me to really get something out of the experience. Obviously, you can get something out of any service activity, even if it is only a one-day event; however, working with an organization on a weekly basis for at least six months not only shows dedication but also will allow you to look at your entire experience, its effects on you, and its effects on the people whose lives you touched. I had heard of the Big Brothers/Big Sisters program, and decided that this would be fun and could fit into my schedule. The experience was difficult and frustrating at first because the young man I was matched with was having difficulties in school and was not fitting in well with his peers. His father had left several years prior, and he had grown up without a male role model. However, towards the end of my two-and-a-half years with him, I began to see some improvement in his attitude and work ethic, and it was truly rewarding to find that I was making an impact on someone's life. My experiences with Big Brothers/Big Sisters were a topic of several of my interview questions.

During my time at the University of Missouri, I was very interested in going on a medical mission. However, as I found out, interest was not all that was needed. Most of the groups I found only wanted doctors or nurses. I searched and e-mailed for nearly a year before finding a group heading to the jungles of Belize that was willing to take me. The organization was Light of the World Missions. Realize however, that organizations change their policies frequently so this group may no longer want to take pre-med students and organizations that in the past would not have wanted an undergraduate student may be more than willing to allow you to join the group. As more and more nonprofit organizations are building web sites, the Internet would be a great place to start searching for groups that go on medical missions. Another great resource is the medical school at your undergraduate institution (or a nearby medical school), as many hospitals have physicians that make yearly trips and may be interested in having a student with them. I had just completed an EMT training course, which may have helped the organization feel more comfortable taking me on the mission. Some sort of medical training may make you more desirable to organizations. Another factor when looking for organizations is fitting their trips into your schedule. I went to Belize during the summer break between my sophomore and junior years.

I was able to get enough donations from the generous members of my church to fund my trip as well as buy supplies to take with me. I ended up with 10 large tubs full of supplies, which I had to take on the cargo part of the plane. Along with a group consisting of a physician and several nurses, I spent nearly two weeks there as I helped build a clinic, taught the people about basic hygiene and medical care, taught the caregivers of each community CPR, took blood pressures, recorded histories, etc.

I enjoyed myself immensely and so decided to do another mission. This time I went with a different group to the mountains of Honduras. This group was led by a local physician whose son went to the same school as I did and he wanted to take a team during his son's spring break. This trip had fewer people so I was able to spend more time with the doctors and a dentist. I was taught how to anesthetize and pull teeth. Many of the people needed whole rows of teeth extracted, and the general surgeon taught me how to suture the gums closed after pulling them all. I learned so much about the people and cultures in both countries just by sitting with them (and the interpreter) and asking them questions. I found that most of the time people do not get offended if you admit to not knowing and ask appropriate questions. In Honduras, I also instructed locals on how to take medications as well as triage the patients waiting in long lines to see the doctors. I learned so much about being a doctor and was able to experience many of the positive aspects of the medical profession.

During college, I was lucky enough to be offered a job working in the inventory department of the operating room at a local private hospital. The hospital was a level two trauma center in a major city with over 30 operating suites. The timing was perfect for me, as they had just consolidated the entire inventory into a central location and needed people to run items to rooms in the middle of cases, keep track of all the items in the room and order anything that was needed. Once the nurses and physicians learned of my interest in medicine, they invited me to watch some cases. I would come in several hours before my shift began to observe some cases. The first case I saw was a coronary artery bypass graft, which was absolutely unbelievable. I began to see more and more cases and eventually got to help out in small ways. I held retractors for major cases, such as total joint replacements, abdominal aortic aneurism repairs, femoral to popliteal artery bypasses, rotator cuff repairs, etc. The physicians for the most part were all nice to me and willing to teach me. This made my experience even more meaningful and really gave me some idea of what I wanted to do once I entered medical school. One of the most important things I learned from the surgical technologists and the nurses, as well as the other staff, was that the medical profession works best as a team. Everyone has different roles and all are essential to accomplishing the goal of providing the best possible care to the patient. Doctors, nurses and administrators all work together and cannot function alone.

If you are not sure a medical career is right for you, take some time off and really sort things out before you commit to applying. Doing some community service projects can not only help you determine if you really want to make the commitment to a life of service, but will also distinguish you from other candidates. Once you start the process, things get hectic and fast-paced and before you know it, you are enrolled in medical school classes. If you were not sure in the first place, and find out you don't like it, you will have just wasted a lot of time, energy and money. Medical schools do not want students who will quit or become unsure if they are willing to commit to the many years of training and hectic lifestyle of a physician; however, having extracurricular activities that have shown you have a good understanding of the demands of the medical profession and that you are able to commit to a service organization will erase any doubt about your motivations and goals. Remember that there will be some major road blocks, but don't let them discourage you. Be unique, and be true to yourself.

--Nathan Mall

GETTING IN

Chapter 5: The MCAT

Chapter 6: Applying

Chapter 7: The Interview

Chapter 8: Financial Aid and Scholarships

Chapter 9: Choosing a Medical School

The MCAT

CHAPTER 5

In the first chapter, we discussed some general information about the MCAT. It may seem daunting, but there are many resources out there to help you ace it. Although there's no surefire way to get that perfect score, prep courses and general study will pull you through. In this chapter, you will learn more about the MCAT, itself and hear how various students attacked the MCAT. They will talk about the pros and cons of Kaplan, Princeton Review, school-offered courses, and studying on your own. The chapter concludes with some basic MCAT advice.

The Basics

The MCAT is composed of four sections: Physical Sciences, Biological Sciences, Verbal Reasoning and the Writing Sample. All of the sections consist of multiple choice questions except for the Writing Sample, which consists of two essays. The number of test questions for each section, the order of the exam sections and the time allotted are as follows:

SECTION	# OF QUESTIONS	TIME (MIN)
Physical Sciences	**52**	**70**
Verbal Reasoning	**40**	**60**
Writing Sample	**2**	**60**
Biological Sciences	**52**	**70**

The Verbal Reasoning section consists of several passages, each about 500 to 600 words long, taken from the "humanities, social sciences, and areas of the natural sciences," which are loosely defined areas. These topics are often not tested elsewhere on the MCAT. Each passage is followed by five to 10 questions based on the information presented in the passage. All of the information needed to answer each question is provided in the accompanying passage so you should not need to apply any outside information you may have studied.

The Physical Sciences section is designed to assess your reasoning in general chemistry and physics. The Biological Sciences section is designed to assess your reasoning in biology and organic chemistry. For a complete list of specific topics covered in each section, check the official MCAT web site at www.aamc.org/mcat. Each section contains 10-11 problem sets, each about 250 words in length that describe a situation or problem. Each problem set is followed by four to eight questions. There are also approximately 10 questions found in each section not accompanied by a passage. Unlike the Verbal Reasoning section, the Physical and Biological Sciences sections do expect you to have a background in these areas and use information you have studied before the test to answer the questions.

The Writing Sample consists of two 30-minute essays. This section of the MCAT is designed to assess your ability to develop a central idea, synthesize concepts and ideas, write clearly, and use proper grammar, syntax and punctuation. Each Writing Sample item provides a specific topic that you must respond to by typing your response. The topics vary widely from your opinions on global warming to whether or not you agree with a common adage, but do not include religious or emotionally charged issues or issues related to the application process or your decision to pursue a career in medicine.

The MCAT is truly a grueling test, but luckily, the total exam length has decreased significantly with the implementation of the computerized format. The overall length of the test day is about five-and-a-half hours. There are three optional 10-minute breaks.

How the MCAT is scored

Your total score on the MCAT is a composite of the score for each of the four sections. For each multiple choice section, your raw score is calculated by adding the number of questions you answer correctly. It is important to note that there is no penalty for incorrect answers, unlike some of the other standardized tests. Since there are multiple versions of the MCAT given at any one time, it is necessary to convert the raw scores to a scale to take this difference into consideration. For the three multiple choice sections of the test, the scaled scores range from a low of 1 to a high of 15. For the writing sample, each of your essays is read by two different individuals. Each individual score ranges from 1 to 6 and the total raw score is then converted to an alphabetic scale ranging from J (lowest) to T (highest). The alphabetic score is obtained from the summation of the scores received on each of your essays.

MCAT resources

It is critical for you to be proactive when preparing for this ever-important test. You should talk to students who have taken the test before you and stay in touch with your pre-medical advisor, if available, to be aware of all upcoming deadlines. The best place to check out the nitty-gritty details of the MCAT is at the official MCAT web site, www.aamc.org/mcat. A practice online test is offered at www.e-mcat.com.

Please note that all of us had to take the old paper-based version of the test. The new computerized format has one-third fewer questions, and is about 30 percent shorter in length.

All data is from the American Association of Medical Colleges web site: www.aamc.org

--Michele Blank and Allen Hwang

The Kaplan Experience

When beginning to prepare for the MCAT, the most important decision you will make is how you are going to allocate your study time. Will you shell out the money to take a review course, and if so, which one? You could study from a book which would run only $50 or take classes that cost $1,600 and literally anything in between. With multiple commercial classes available, in addition to university-sponsored courses and do-it-yourself review books, how do you choose the method that is right for you? After pondering the options as a college junior, I chose to use the Kaplan Test Prep Company.

The primary reason I benefited from Kaplan was that it provided many opportunities to become familiar with the MCAT format. The MCAT was different than any other test I had ever taken, but after completing the six full-length practice exams that Kaplan administered, I felt extremely comfortable during the actual test. Available only at the centers themselves, Kaplan has over 30 additional tests and subject-specific passages, all with detailed answers, so there is more practice material than you could ever complete. To me, these practice materials were the most important aspect of the course, and well worth my $1,600.

The other aspect of Kaplan that appealed to me was the length of the course. Considering my study habits, I knew that if I tried to study on my own or even take the four-session school course, I would wait until a week before the test to start preparing. The Kaplan curriculum lasts for about three months and consists of two three-hour classes each week with practice exams on Saturdays. The course is time-intensive, but it helped me stay focused. Furthermore, Kaplan's classes and review books cover only information that has appeared on past MCATs, providing a complete but not an excessive amount of study material.

In my opinion, the biggest difference between a commercial and a school-sponsored program is the overall purpose of the course. Most university courses are designed to provide the information necessary to adequately prepare for the MCAT, whereas classes such as Kaplan and Princeton Review focus on developing test-taking skills in addition to presenting the basic science information. Kaplan focuses heavily on "breaking down" MCAT passages and questions in order for students to better determine the intent of the question and identify key information, while eliminating wrong answers. When I initially signed up to take the Kaplan course, I thought the acquisition of these skills would help increase my score. About halfway through the course, however, I realized that although the test-taking suggestions were intended to help students better understand the passage material, they were not useful to me without extensive knowledge of the information presented in the passage. You may find the test-taking insights helpful; however, I do not recommend taking a course solely to enhance your testing skills since learning the material is crucial.

Kaplan has other disadvantages as well. First and foremost, it is not cheap. As of 2006, the entire classroom course costs $1,549, which includes classes, materials and practice tests. However, remember that you are about to pay up to $50,000 per year to attend medical school. In comparison, the cost of an MCAT course is relatively inexpensive. Second, Kaplan instructors are often students who recently completed the MCAT. They do not always possess a complete understanding of the material, but they are willing to spend the time to help you answer any questions. Finally, since the Kaplan course focused on test-taking skills, I felt the actual scientific information was often underemphasized. If you choose to pay for a commercial course, remember that the MCAT primarily tests factual knowledge, so you must take the time to memorize the information. The Kaplan books are good sources for this information, rather than the classes.

The Kaplan course, like any of the other MCAT study aides, has advantages and disadvantages. I liked Kaplan because I felt like the course complemented my studying preferences. The best advice I can give is to determine what you want to get out of a review course and make a decision based on your desired goals. If you are motivated enough to sit yourself down a few months ahead of time and begin studying, you may not need a course. However, Kaplan made the process easier for me, since it forced me to start studying early. The books they supply were very helpful for the basic science material, and the practice tests were vital in preparing me for the real thing.

—Mark Neely

The Princeton Review Course

When it comes to studying for the MCAT, there are three options. One, don't study and use the test to prove you're as intelligent as you always thought you were. Two, plan your own study schedule and use your old textbooks or a study guide from the local bookstore. Three, sign up for a review course where you are "forced" to come to class, you take practice exams in simulated test environments, and instructors tell you all the material you need to know (and what not to bother with). For those of us who need a little motivation to study for the MCAT and feel hopelessly overwhelmed looking at the stack of old physics, chemistry, and biology textbooks, a review course is a great (although sometimes pricey) option.

I opted to take a review course offered by The Princeton Review. There are different options for courses, such as online, private tutoring, and regular classroom courses. As of 2006, the price for the typical classroom course was $1,599, but this can vary depending on location. I chose The Princeton Review classroom course for a number of reasons. First, the study guides they provided were extensive and helpful. We were given workbooks with chapters describing all the key concepts and workbooks with corresponding sample exam questions. We also received multiple practice exams which could be taken on our own time, and other exams which were administered on weekends at the course site under simulated testing conditions. After all, one of the most difficult things about the MCAT is being able to concentrate for hours at a time! I've heard that not all courses let you keep your workbooks or sample exams, but with The Princeton Review we got to keep it all (except for a couple of practice exams).

In addition to the course materials, The Princeton Review holds courses that are taught by mostly college students or recent graduates who have taken the MCAT, scored well, and undergone a training course run by The Princeton Review. Although all instructors have high scores on the MCAT, the quality of the instructors varies widely. Sometimes you get a really bright student who knows all the material but can't quite seem to explain it. Sometimes you get a recent college graduate who really understands how to convey the important concepts to you and how to explain useful shortcuts for the exam. Other times you might not be so lucky. Unfortunately, my course was filled with instructors that I did not find helpful. I felt that the course was poorly organized such that many times no instructors showed up for class at all. We didn't have a chemistry instructor assigned until the last third of the course, so we rushed through all of that material in the last few weeks before the MCAT instead of spreading it out over the length of the entire course.

Furthermore, some of the instructors seemed like they had no interest in teaching and just boasted of how much they were being paid for doing so little work. I felt like attending the classes was a waste of time and that I would have gained much more in a shorter amount of time if I had just looked at the study materials on my own.

Although the instructors assigned to teach me didn't seem interested in teaching, I do have friends who have taught for The Princeton Review and have invested much time and effort in preparing for their classes. So it really just comes down to the instructors that happen to be assigned in your area. I suggest asking people who have taken the course before about how their instructors were and asking The Princeton Review if those instructors will be returning. If you aren't a classroom learner or if you have doubts about the quality of the instructors, then I suggest you just try to acquire the study materials that are available in bookstores. Unfortunately, the more extensive review books are only available from those who have taken the class.

If you still think you need to attend classes and be lectured to, The Princeton Review has numerous options ranging from book sets to classroom tutoring to even personal tutoring. I chose the Hyperlearning course where classes met three times a week in the evenings and on both Saturdays and Sundays (Sundays are generally practice exam days). The course began in late January and finished the week before the April MCAT. The Hyperlearning format is great for those who are better at intensive short-term learning. It's a little difficult to manage if you have a lot of schoolwork or extracurricular activities, but it seemed like the perfect option for the summer. More traditional courses that meet less often and cover a wider span of time are also offered at Princeton Review.

To summarize, first figure out how you learn best and then decide whether you feel like you should take a review course or not. The Princeton Review has great study materials, but the quality of instruction really varies, so check it out carefully before you plop down $1,600 on the course.

—Emily Eads

The Cheaper Route: School-Offered MCAT Courses

When I sat down to think about studying for the MCAT, it was the spring semester of my junior year and I was doing 12 hours of work-study, attending 20 hours of class, and studying countless hours each week. I tried to figure out the best, most relaxed schedule for reviewing for the MCAT. However, since I am a self-proclaimed masochist, I decided to take the test at the end of the semester.

Knowing how busy my schedule was and how limited my funds were, taking a Kaplan or Princeton Review MCAT prep course was never an option for me. I didn't think about the exam until about three months before I was scheduled to take it, and I wanted to spend the minimal amount of time studying that would allow me to get double-digit scores in each of the sections. Given my time constraints, I decided to attend MCAT review sessions held by faculty members at Grinnell College (in Grinnell, IA).

At the first review meeting, each student took a full-length MCAT exam from a previous year. The practice test was administered exactly as the actual exam would be, and the faculty graded the exams and scored them so that we would have a rough idea of our starting level of knowledge. Before the MCAT, the last multiple choice standardized exam I had taken was the SAT. Taking this practice exam before studying reminded me of the format used and depth of knowledge required for standardized exams.

Once a week for the next four weeks, faculty members from the biology and chemistry departments and the director of the college's writing lab held one-hour review sessions on their respective areas of expertise. At each of these sessions, the faculty member in charge would hand out sample problems from previous exams and the students would attempt the questions on their own before going through the answers with the faculty. The questions were selected to represent the main areas that would be tested. Although we didn't actually review very much material as a group, these sessions were helpful in identifying which subjects I already knew, and which subjects I should review. The session I found most helpful was the one on writing the essays for the MCAT exam. Writing college essays for three years, I had been used to incorporating a lot of fluff and flowery words into my writing. However, for the MCAT essays I found it easier to follow the standard style and format that, although quite dry, fulfilled the essay requirements more efficiently.

After having identified the subjects that I was rusty at, I used a Kaplan book that I bought in a bookstore to review specific areas. Given my limited amount of time to study, I didn't review areas I was already confident about and only looked at the material that I was completely unfamiliar with. During the next two months, I only spent a total of about six hours reviewing. In March, the faculty administered another full-length practice exam. I used this test to try a few test-taking strategies that I was considering using on the real exam. For instance, I found it helpful to glance at the verbal questions before reading the accompanying text.

Overall, the most efficient and helpful form of studying for me was taking the two full-length practice exams. The MCAT is a long test and is both mentally and physically tiring. Yet when the time came for the real exam, I was prepared for the long day ahead having sat through the simulated experience twice already. Because there are also a lot of conflicting test-taking strategies out there such as winging it, using a book, taking a class or getting a private tutor, attempting different strategies on a practice exam let me identify which strategies worked for me.

The MCAT tests a vast amount of material, and it is simply impossible to prepare for everything that may be on the exam. If you have very little time to study, I advise you to take as many practice exams as you can. Practice questions can help identify which areas should be reviewed, and simply figuring out why you missed certain questions is a great way to review key concepts. Since the MCAT exam is longer than most other standardized exams, you need to see how it will feel to take at least one full-length practice test. Sitting through five hours of multiple-choice-hell on a Saturday, whether it's for a practice or real exam, is also a great excuse to head straight to the pub…as though one needs an excuse to go to the pub.

—*Sarah Evans*

Making It on Your Own

Call me crazy, but the way I saw it, you should not need to take out your first medical school loan just to take the MCAT. I did not happen to have $1,000 lying around my dorm room, so I decided against taking a preparatory course. My decision was difficult and relatively frightening considering that the success of my future career potentially hung in the balance. In the end I decided that I could effectively motivate and discipline myself, structure my own review and balance my other school work as I did so. But you should do a careful self-assessment before you decide to forgo taking a preparatory class. The fact that so many pre-med students take and recommend a course of some sort is evidence that many do not feel they can manage a study schedule independently. While there is something to be said for having an organized and experience-tested course to lead you through the process, I did not find one necessary, nor do I regret my decision to venture out on my own.

I started my MCAT review three months before the test day (which is about when review courses start). For $15, I bought a Barron's MCAT review book that included test-taking tips, outlines and brief details for the major topics that I was expected to understand for the exam, and multiple full-length practice exams. In retrospect, I recommend that you make sure you buy a really good review book; mine contained only rudimentary descriptions and explanations of the test topics. I started by reading through the review book and identifying the areas with which I had the most trouble. After one month of somewhat casual review, I suddenly realized that I had a lot more to study than seemed possible. The realization was somewhat demoralizing and frightening, which leads me to my next point.

Fear can be a powerful motivator. Once I had come to terms with my panic, I was ready to begin my real review, but now I had only two months of study before the test. If you happen to get one of the review books that actually describes and explains topics, it might be sufficient for you to do most of your studying right from the prep book. However, I found that for topics that I did not remember from my previous coursework, it was better for me to refer to textbooks and use my review book as a guide to which topics were important and which were irrelevant. I found it useful to break down my review by week: each week I studied a different one of the four main subjects. After I reviewed my weak areas in each subject, I did practice problems from the book to find out what areas I was still unsure about. I worked on practice problems throughout my review, gradually increasing the number of problems and working to increase the rate of problem-solving as I progressed. No matter where I was in my studying, I made sure always to check the practice exams carefully and understand what I got wrong and why it was wrong (not just what the right answer was).

This brings me to practice MCAT exams. The most useful thing I did was take several full-length exams. If your review book does not have enough practice exams, it is worthwhile to invest in extras. It was extremely painful to lock myself in a library study room when it was a beautiful spring Saturday outside. Yet practicing taking the full-length test was absolutely invaluable. Official MCAT prep courses do the same thing, but they have proctors and will grade your test for you. I recommend that when you are practicing that you follow the time constraints, take only the allotted breaks between sections, avoid interruptions and grade your exam carefully. Get a feel for how fast you have to work, how tired you will get by the Biological Sciences section, how much caffeine you can tolerate and how you should react when you become stuck in the middle of a section. Believe it or not, screaming obscenities is not a condoned response, so you should work on alternative approaches to relieve your stress and revive your concentration.

Finally, I stopped studying a week or so before the exam. Some would say I lost motivation and gave up, but I like to pretend that I learned all there was for me to know. Whatever delusion you can create for yourself, I recommend taking a little time off before the exam. Last minute cramming will leave you stressed and mentally drained, so don't do it. Relax and enjoy your last days. The MCAT is only the beginning!

—Claire Sandstrom

I did not take the MCAT as an undergraduate because I was a double major and because I took some of the pre-med classes in a less-than-organized fashion. So the exam ended up getting delegated to the summer after my senior year instead. There I was, graduated, supposedly knowledgeable about everything I needed to do well on the MCAT, and I felt like I knew practically nothing once again. Had I really taken physics? Since I couldn't remember the answer to that question and others with satisfying clarity, a major dilemma for me was whether to take one of the MCAT courses I kept hearing raves about.

I asked professors, friends and people I knew who were already in or through medical school how I should study for the MCAT. Basically, I gathered that the review course is a good option in that it spreads the subjects out, teaches test-taking strategies and provides several practice exams along the way. So taking the review course would be a wise decision if I felt like I would not be able to manage my own time or get my hands on practice exams. However, my decision was to buy a Kaplan review book, study on my own and forgo the course. I saved quite a bit of money, I felt like I prepared really well on my own, and I never regretted my decision.

That summer I worked full-time, so I had to balance my time between a physically tiring job and studying. I gave myself slightly less than three months to study, and took the two weeks off from my job before the exam for an intense, final preparatory period. My pre-med club was fantastic. A group of students from school who wanted to go into medicine set up a couple Saturdays for taking a practice MCAT in a controlled setting so that we could get used to the timing involved. Practicing the MCAT in advance was probably my saving grace. Timing, I discovered, was everything. I bombed the first practice test I took because I had no idea how carefully I needed to monitor my time and I did not finish. It was a very sobering experience, but thankfully it got easier with every practice test.

My mantra became, "take as many practice tests as you can." I cannot stress how important this was for me. Knowing the format of the exam cold, understanding all of the sections, how many questions each has and how much time to devote to each question made a huge difference in the outcome. I looked at practice statements for the writing samples and worked on organizing essays so that I could do it reasonably efficiently and quickly while keeping the quality of my writing solid.

Sure, in the end I sacrificed a lot of fun time for study time. Adding insult to injury, it was disgustingly glorious outside on my MCAT exam day, as I discovered during our short lunch break. The knots in my stomach were still there, and nothing made that day any easier to take; but I got through it. Looking back during medical school, the sacrifices I made to prepare for the MCAT are not hard to bear at all. So I did not need to take the review course because I knew how I wanted to organize my time, what I wanted to study, and I had a lot of advice on how to go about doing it. I believe that taking that review course would have wasted my time and could even have been detrimental by taking away more study hours, especially since I was working full-time.

—Susan Harley

Retaking the MCAT

"So you want to retake the MCAT?" My pre-med advisor looked at me disapprovingly. Then he pulled out the AAMC booklet from his desk drawer and opened it to a table with data on people who had retaken the MCAT. Based on their initial score, the table showed what percentage of the students got a higher, lower or the same score. The data was not promising at all for my score level.

When medical schools receive MCAT scores, the results of all recently taken exams are sent automatically. In other words, you cannot choose which one of your scores to send to medical schools. Therefore it is wise to take the MCAT only when you feel ready for it. Yet even after substantial preparation, the results you get may not be as good as the results you want.

The decision to retake the MCAT is one that really depends on the individual. It depends on why you think the first try did not go as well as you thought and whether you think you have a reasonable chance of changing the circumstances for the next test. Generally, you do no have to explain this to a school because many students do this, but admission committees do not look favorably upon falling or unchanging scores. For me, I was satisfied with all of the sections except for the Biological Sciences section. I also knew the reason why: I overestimated how much organic chemistry I remembered from my sophomore year. Mine was a specific problem with a specific solution: I had to relearn orgo! Most advisers will tell you that if you cannot pinpoint a specific reason for doing poorly on the first exam (e.g., you were not feeling well during the test or there was one section you didn't study enough for), chances are you score will not improve by that much. Given my situation, and the fact that I knew of a specific problem, I went ahead and studied and retook the MCAT. It worked for me; my Biological Sciences score went up from an acceptable range to a competitive one and my scores in the other sections were maintained.

Although I retook the MCAT, I would not recommend it for everyone. For example, don't retake the MCAT if you think that the score will go up simply because this is your second time or because you took some advanced biology course that you assume will automatically bring up your score. In addition, do not be a perfectionist. If you have a 30 something score, you may not want to risk getting a lower score on the retest provided—they won't tabulate the highest score from each section. Be practical as well. The MCAT is meant to be hard for everyone and medical schools know that, so while you may think your score is not good enough, it might be acceptable for admission. Acceptable scores depend on the institution. In general, and there are definitely exceptions, state schools will accept scores lower than 30 while more competitive research oriented schools require scores above 30.

There are several situations, however, in which retaking the MCAT may be beneficial. Maybe you studied on your own for the first time and you think you would benefit from the structured organization of commercial MCAT courses. Conversely, if you took a course and think it took away from your productive time, you may do better the second time if you think you can study hard and efficiently on your own. Or maybe you just had a bad day on the test day and did not perform to your maximum level. Finally, maybe you are like me: your weakness is in a specific area that you think you can improve on.

The bottom line is to make sure that you have a specific reason why you think your score will improve the second time around. Assess your own strengths and weaknesses. Do not be intimidated by the statistics. At the end of the day, tables, counselors and books cannot predict anything about the performance of any one individual; it is only you who knows yourself.

—Parvin Fatheddin

MCAT Advice

Take classes. I don't mean review course classes. I am speaking of academic classes offered at nearly every college in the nation. There were a few classes that I found especially helpful for the MCAT. For the Physical Sciences section, I recommend two semesters of physics and two semesters of general chemistry. For the Biological Sciences section, I recommend physiology and one semester of biochemistry, which are not required to apply to medical school (although some medical schools do recommend taking biochemistry). You should also take your required organic chemistry courses. These few core classes should help to prepare you for the MCAT. If you are an overachiever or actually enjoy science classes, there are a few other classes that I felt were helpful (but not necessary) for the MCAT, such as genetics, evolution and psychology. Of course, the more classes you take, the better. This may seem like quite a few courses, but again, many are already requirements for applying for medical school.

Now, this plan of coursework is not without its problems. First, it takes a lot of time. It will take one to two years of heavy studying rather than a few weeks in an intensive training class. Second, it takes a lot of time. It is a scientific fact that by the time you finish your last class, exactly enough time will have passed for you to forget absolutely everything that you have learned. It is true. I have experienced it.

There are ways to prevent these time problems, however. First, get started early. Sign up for these classes early enough so that you will have taken them and had enough time to review by the time you take the MCAT. Second, don't sell your books for pizza money. It may seem like a lot of money, but it doesn't match the $1,000 you spend on an MCAT review program when you realize that you have no study materials.

Now, about actually studying for the science sections. I do recommend that you go out and buy an MCAT books that you like. Most actually provide very good overviews of the topics and materials that you will need to know. I know it's another expense, but again, $1,000 is more than $30. Use these as guides, not references. Your unsold textbooks will be your references. Go over the review book topic by topic, being sure that you understand each major theme. If you don't get something, refer to your textbook. If you still don't understand, ask your professor. Lather, rinse, repeat. Continue this cycle of reviewing topics until you feel comfortable with as much as your brain can hold.

The Verbal Reasoning section is a tough section for which to study. Unlike the science sections, there is not a discrete amount of material that you can memorize or understand. My advice is to read a ton. And not comic books, but magazines, books and newspapers. Check out your local paper and graduate to fancier publications such as *Newsweek*, *Time*, *Atlantic Monthly* and *The New York Times*. The best way to master the reading section is to read widely. And don't just gloss over what you read, but think critically about what you're reading. What is the author saying? How is he/she saying it? Do I agree? Critical reading skills come only with practice.

Now that you've got the knowledge and skills for the MCAT, practice taking it. Many times. Practice tests are everywhere, many of which are free. Ask around and you'll find that some of your friends may have copies of old practice tests or even the AAMC-published old tests. If all else fails, go out and buy some or see your career counseling office if you have one. I recommend taking at least five practice tests, and not in bits and pieces. Taking one section at a time is like training for the marathon by running 26 miles in 10 feet increments. Sit down and force yourself to sit through all of it. This way, the real test will be the same old same old by the time you get to it, and that's a good thing. You want to be able to concentrate on the test questions, not the format or the length or the funny twitch you get on your face by the sixth hour.

When test day is approaching, there are a few things I would recommend. First, go to your test site a day or two before and find out where you will park and where the exact location of your exam will be. This will prevent a lot of unnecessary stress the day of the exam. On test day itself, make sure you give yourself plenty of time to reach your site. Nothing ruins an MCAT day quite like getting pulled over for speeding to the test center (yes, I know someone who got a ticket, and no, he wasn't happy about it). During the exam itself, remember that there is no penalty for guessing. Answer every single question, even if you have no idea what the answer is. Finally, try your best to relax. After all, it's only a test.

Applying

CHAPTER 6

Having already endured a year of organic chemistry, a year of physics, volunteer engagements, hours in the laboratory and who knows what else, you might think that applying will be a piece of cake. Think again. Filling out the application is the most important step towards receiving the acceptance letter.

The Bottom Line

What matters the most is whether or not the admissions committee will see you in the application that you submit. They have to go through thousands of these every year; in 2005 there were 37,364 medical school applicants and 17,004 of those matriculated, and everybody has taken the prerequisites, so you should not count on the A in organic chemistry to make your application stand out. Your MCAT score(s) and your transcript(s) are there to demonstrate that you can do the work and have the mental capacity to soak in the tremendous amount of information that will be poured over you once you are in medical school. A brilliant and outstanding application can land you a secondary application and even an interview at many schools. Before you start applying, here are some things that I think you should keep in mind.

Start early

I cannot stress enough how important it is to start as soon as you can. There is nothing enjoyable about spending the last minutes of midnight deadlines frantically proofreading your essays. If you are anything like I am, you take care of things as they come along, which is to say that you assign priority based solely on the deadline. This is not a very good idea when it comes to filling out the application, simply because it will take you hours—or more likely, days—to transfer all the remarkable things you have done onto paper. The earlier you start working on your application, the less your stress level will be, and the more time you will have to make your application just perfect, not to mention the greater your chances are of getting accepted by a school with a rolling admissions policy, which includes majority of medical schools. The earliest you can submit the application is early June, so you should start working on your application in May and plan on wrapping things up sometime in June.

Fill out the forms

To get an idea of what is really required of you, you should log on to AAMC (www.aamc.org/students/amcas/start.htm) as soon as they post the application in early May and set up your username and passwords. If everything is already set up, you are more likely to log on and work on your application when you have a few minutes to kill. I suggest that you then head out to the local coffee shop, bookstore, library or your own room and start a list that will include dates and a couple of points that you want to emphasize regarding your jobs, volunteering experiences, laboratory experiences, extracurricular activities, publications, awards and/or anything else that you think will help the admission committee get an idea of who you are. Don't underestimate your achievements. Just because you did not win a medal at some competition is not a reason not to mention somewhere on your application that you participated in such and such competition. When you are not sure whether something is worth mentioning or not, ask yourself how many pre-meds have done a similar thing or consult your college advisers. Keep in mind that if you do not mention it on paper, the admission committee members will never know about it. I would also strongly advise that you designate a folder, electronic or paper, into which you will stuff everything from the list you have started, to your unofficial transcripts and your essay drafts.

Some secondary applications are done online, just as the AMCAS. But for those that are not, be sure to find a typewriter you can use to fill out the applications and get familiar with how to use it. Being able to type things on the small lines of the application takes time and practice. You want to make your application look as professional as possible, so get to know your typewriter before you make the first mark on an actual application.

Know your deadlines!

Set your priorities straight and know the deadlines. I suggest you double-check the deadlines. If there are discrepancies between the deadline that is listed on the AAMC web site and the one that is on the school's web site, call the school and check. Also, when making plans for the summer and drawing up your schedule for the fall semester, do so with the application deadlines in mind. I did not start working on my application until late in the summer, which meant that I did most of the work on my application during the fall semester. I was not planning ahead and it was difficult to juggle a demanding class schedule with writing the application. This is also the time when I should have stopped to think about what was more important—making an A on a term paper or making a deadline for a medical school that I was interested in attending. Make wise choices when forced to decide between polishing the midterm paper and spending several hours polishing the application. However hard it may be to submit a substandard term paper, it is better than submitting a substandard AMCAS application. Same goes for the deadline. As I said, regardless of how hard you have worked and how remarkable your achievements, they cannot get you into medical school until they are on paper and at the disposal of the admission committee members by the appropriate time.

In a nutshell, remember the importance of starting early, being aware of the time demands and deadlines, and most importantly figuring out how to use the application to present yourself in writing so that you are invited to present yourself in person.

—Ivana Nikolic

Writing Your Essay

Unlike your check made payable to AMCAS, your application essay will not simply disappear after being dropped in the mailbox. Instead, this pesky component of your application will be chewed up by committees, digested and hopefully regurgitated in your lap during resultant interviews. Secondary applications tend to ask targeted essay questions, making topic selection easier, so conquering the open-ended essay question will be my focus. This is how I chose my AMCAS "personal statement" topic, edited my writing, found helpful feedback and dealt with the consequences.

As with any essay, selecting a topic is the first step. It seemed to me that this "personal statement" should convey something about my motivation to attend medical school. This little science major, however, was not passionate about any particular aspect of medicine; I just thought I might enjoy it more than my other post-graduation options. So I chose to predicate my argument with the existence of some personal uncertainty, and I believe complete honesty worked in my favor.

The first paragraph needs to introduce the topic and reach a thesis of sorts. In my case, the essay was based on a letter I had written months before. While writing to a doctor about finding some summertime medical-exposure, a first draft turned into a spontaneous exploration of what sorts of things I enjoy doing and why. The first paragraph of my personal statement recounted this story and concluded, "45 minutes later I was left with a list of character traits and personal quirks that I thought would make a good doctor. I hope you will agree."

The substance of my essay approached a number of my hobbies, like raising orchids, giving tours of caves and performing, from the standpoint that I only thrive when eliciting growth and feedback from my surroundings. Each paragraph presented a personal interest and analyzed it with regard to being a content physician. Perhaps the hardest part was addressing my volunteerism in an operating room, which I found rather passive and boring. I presented this negative impression, but justified it by saying that I prefer doing, or at least learning, over being a spectator. This essay successfully relayed my interest in medicine because I actually convinced myself to go to medical school in the process of first conceiving it. It was honest, active, and with enough work, it became well-organized.

Once you formulate an argument, you need to be particularly careful that you have said everything just right. This entails multiple proofreadings on different days as well as seeking second opinions. Respected professors and pre-med advisors are ideal for final revisions and advice. I remember one secondary essay that required me to write 500 new words on the same topic I selected for my AMCAS personal statement. In such troubling cases, seeking professional advice can be helpful. In this instance, I found consultation with a college English professor invaluable.

Finally, your words will make their last stand at the interview. I made a habit of reading all pertinent essays the night before each big day. Since they really know little else about you, interviewers are prone to focusing on parts of your essays they found praiseworthy or troublesome. In one extreme case, I spent a full hour discussing orchids with a dean of admissions who shared this interest. Other interviewers may not understand you and your essay as well, but if you remember what you wrote, and hold your ground, you will at least appear confident in your beliefs.

Try to have your applications essays present an analytical process, rather than state mere facts or desires. Remember to leave plenty to time to proofread, and be sure everything you wrote is fresh in your mind for the interview.

—Mike Malinzak

Getting Those Recommendations

Every aspect of your medical school application is important, including your recommendations. Solid, enthusiastic recommendations can make you stand out and enhance your application.

Unfortunately, I didn't realize this until it was too late. In college, I avoided interacting with my professors at nearly all costs. I sat in the back of the classroom and was one of the first out of the door when class ended. If I ever came to class early, I read the newspaper. I was confident I could ask my professors if I had any questions about the course material, but other than that I saw no need to approach them.

When it was time for me to request recommendations for my medical school applications, I quickly realized that things were far from perfect. Our pre-med advisor wanted us to have a minimum of three recommendations: two science related and one non-science related. I had studied a foreign language in a small group setting for two years with the same professor, so I was confident she would write positively about me. I had also been working in a research laboratory for the past one and a half years, and felt I had really connected with my research mentor. Thus, my research mentor provided my second recommendation.

That was it. I didn't have a third recommendation, and I had no idea what to do. I tried thinking of all of the science classes I had taken, and whether I had even talked to the professor. For every class, the result was the same. If I was lucky, I made eye contact with the professor once or twice. Any letter he wrote was bound to be to the effect of "Maheer was a good student. He got this grade in my class. That's all I know about him." Figuring it was a lost cause, I approached the professor of my physics recitation section, since he was a great teacher and had a dry wit that I admired. To my surprise, he took an hour or so of his time to try to get to know me. While that hour may have given him a better picture of what kind of person I was, it was no substitute for having a recommendation from a person who was actually familiar with me.

What does this mean in terms of getting recommendations? I advise that you think about them well before you actually apply. Every class you take and every endeavor in which you participate has the potential to produce an amazing recommendation. That being said, I don't think you should try and amass recommendations from every professor in every class that you have taken. Moreover, I don't think you should schmooze with a professor after class just so he can write you a recommendation in the future. Find a few people who can speak for your abilities and your character, not just your grades. If you do find yourself in my situation, don't panic. You'll be surprised at how willing professors are to write recommendations, even if they don't know you. They will probably want some more information about you, and hopefully will want to meet with you. Granted these recommendations won't be as strong as from someone who actually knows you. But, the bottom line is you'll get your recommendations, one way or another. So, don't worry.

After I had talked to my physics professor for my third recommendation, I was left with the feeling that I had wasted an opportunity to get to know someone who seemed to be really interesting. I think that sort of sentiment should guide your interactions with professors. If something about a professor appeals to you, go and talk to him/her. The conversation does not have to be academically related. Let your interests guide you. It could lead to a much stronger relationship between you and your professor. Also, small settings like seminar classes give you a chance to get to know your professor on more of an individual basis. Take advantage of these types of opportunities, for they tend to be rewarding even if you don't make friends with your instructor. Remember that you don't need to get all your recommendations from your professors. Most schools will tell you explicitly how many letters of recommendation they need from professors. The rest can come from those with whom you have volunteered, done research or anyone else who you feel knows you well. A lot of quality interactions exist and, if you are willing, there are ample opportunities to find them.

—Maheer Gandhavadi

Dealing with Stress

The year that I applied to medical school was particularly stressful, given the implementation of the new online AMCAS application. (Prior to the online application, students would complete their applications on a floppy disk format and return it to AMCAS.) Like many other applicants, I encountered several problems in using the online form and had to spend an excessive amount of time making sure that my application was properly submitted. To add insult to injury, I was completing my application on a dial-up modem with a six-hour time difference from Sub-Saharan Africa where I was doing research towards my master's degree. Although the AAMC has substantially improved the efficiency of the AMCAS online application, the medical school admissions season is much longer and more strenuous than the college admissions process.

Fortunately, I found that much of the stress that the admissions process provoked could be anticipated and therefore reduced to some degree. There are roughly two kinds of stress that exist in each of the four major stages of the admissions process: MCAT preparation, completing AMCAS/personal statement and secondaries, interviewing and making your final decision of school to attend

I would characterize the stress of completing each of the four major stages of applying to medical school as similar in quality to the stress that precedes final exams, completing a term paper or giving a presentation. However, the total duration of the process is much longer lasting, taking almost a complete year from start to finish (that is, if you take your MCAT the April before you apply and receive most of your admissions decisions by March or so). I also found that this stress could be a bit overwhelming at times. After all, while a bad term paper or final exam can be made up for in one way or another, the admissions process really represents for many people the culmination of their educational experience to-date and their desire for a particular type of career and lifestyle. I found it helpful to rely on the same type of relaxing activities that I had always used, e.g., exercise, venting to friends and family, movies, etc. and encourage every applicant to rely on his/her own tried and true methods.

As I received both encouraging and discouraging news from schools, I found it best not to get attached to any one school but to develop a list of my top five schools. After all, it was unlikely that only one school offered the kind of program that would prepare me to meet my career goals. So don't put all of your eggs in one basket.

Talking with friends and family about your concerns and good news is also a great source of stress relief, particularly if they are friends or classmates who are not pre-meds. I found that having many pre-med friends at times was more stressful because they were also concerned about their prospects for getting into a particular school. Finally, I found it useful to take all advice and commentary about my chances for admission to a school with a grain of salt. There is so much folklore related to the admissions process; thus, it is helpful to separate fact from fiction—or at least to be patient until you receive an absolute acceptance or denial letter—before becoming overly invested in either happiness or despair. For instance, I have a friend who interviewed at Northwestern University's Feinberg School of Medicine. When she got to the interview, she shared with one of her fellow interviewees her excitement at having gotten an interview. To which he remarked, "I don't know why you are so happy, I was here for an interview last year." Clearly, displaying his chagrin at having been declined admission the year prior. Similarly, I have a classmate who was invited to interview on the very last day of scheduled interviews at Duke (around February). I was invited to interview at the very beginning of the scheduled interview season (around October) and yet, we are both MD candidates here. Remember, it isn't over until it is over.

In terms of stress more related to the procedural aspects of completing the application and interviews successfully—meeting application deadlines, arranging costly travel arrangements, making sure that you schedule your interviews at a time that does not conflict with pending school or work commitments, etc., organization is key. The summer that I began applying, I bought myself a personal planner to chart all of my important dates. I also created a spreadsheet with a series of checklists for every school to chart when I had communicated with them, when I received notification that they received my scores, application, recommendations, etc. Remember, this process is really a whole year of deadlines that must be integrated into your normal school, work and social schedule. There is some truth to the saying "Never let them see you sweat." After all, as a future medical student and doctor, you will be in countless stressful situations, so admissions officers, interviewers and pre-med advisors will understand if you are a bit nervous. However, they will expect that you can keep a cool head, appear confident and speak intelligently about yourself and your work. I found it helpful to arrive at the city where I was interviewing the night before, so that I could get good sleep, grab a good meal and have time to find my way to the interview. Comfortable dress clothes and a warm coat (because many interviews are held in the winter time) also help!

—Adepeju Gbadebo

The Interview

CHAPTER 7

By the time you have your interview, the respective school already has your MCAT score, GPA and a list of your plethora of extracurricular activities. So what else do they want to know? It's all already there, right?

The interview is the medical school's way of assessing a student's personality and how this personality will fit into the environment of that particular institution. From my experiences hanging out with my fellow first-year medical school students, I must emphasize to you that there is no one particular, prototypical med student personality for which the interviewer is looking. The interviewer will not deduct "points" if you are a naturally reserved person or if you are generally extroverted.

Interview Advice

Being honest to yourself and your personality is the most important piece of advice I can give to you. In your own heart, you know why you want to be a physician, and the only way you can express this desire to the interviewer is by allowing him or her to interact with the real you. My best interviews were those when the interviewer and I just gelled and conversed freely, and I was able to show the interviewer my real personality. Now, not all interviewers conduct interviews in such a free-flowing manner. There will be many interviews that are organized more like a Q&A session. Again, be honest. When I was asked a question I did not know, I made no qualms about it and simply said, "I don't know." Besides compassion, two qualities that I know I look for in my own physician are integrity and honesty.

Now I can get down to the details. Firstly, know the name of the school that you are interviewing at. Sounds idiotic, right? Trust me, it happens. You will be traveling around the country doing interviews one after the other, and a lot of times you will truly be disoriented. Just the other day, my friend who was interviewing in New York told me she was at Columbia and repeatedly said that "she loved it here at Albert Einstein." Not good.

Second, the interviewers are choosing compassionate, intelligent and honest students for the medical profession, so it is in your best interest to dress like a professional. If you are a man, wear a suit and tie. If you are a woman, wear a pant suit or a skirt suit.

I would also recommend that you learn how prone you are to fidgeting in nervous situations. For example, I had my friend interview me while I was in full interview attire. I learned that I tended to tug on my tie and shift my hands restlessly when asked tough questions. Some interviewers like to throw curveballs trying to bump you out of your comfort zone. They may ask you difficult ethical questions or even geography questions out of the blue. Make sure that you stay composed. If you do not have a clue to what the difference in the American and English health care system is, tell him or her so. It seems quite twisted of them to torture you like this, but they are testing how you react to tough situations in which you do not know the solution, something that happens every day as a practicing physician.

The third and last piece of advice I can give you is to come into each interview prepared. This does not mean that you should have a concocted answer for every question that they list on those med school interview web sites. But you do need to make preparations so that you can respond to general questions about yourself because that is what each interviewer is really quizzing you on—whether you know who you are as a person. If you conduct research, you should know what you did, how you did it and the implications your research. Know who you are and become confident in that person.

--Arthur Wu

Telling People What They Want to Hear

In my interview with the former director of research himself, he had just asked me to tell him everything about my research. Somehow I could tell my answer would be one of the very few that mattered to him. At the beginning of the day, the dean of admissions raved to me about this interviewer, and I had spent the rest of my visit hearing about multi-million-dollar research facilities and the perks of a mandatory thesis. Interviewing at a school whose ivy vines dated back to before the American Revolution, I knew that it took both itself and its research very seriously.

Unfortunately, I did not. My first three years of college had spun by in blur of labs, PowerPoint presentations and journal reading. I had sacrificed many hours to the gods of research—pipetting, pouring, spinning, sorting and even falling asleep once or twice on a microscope. Three years and three summers I spent in some sort of research or another. I searched for the drive that kept my colleagues in lab till dawn despite families waiting for them at home. I sought the passion that enabled them to have animated conversations about signaling molecules the same way some fans talked about their favorite sports teams. I was interested by my work—at times I was even engaged. But I never shared this passion for research. After nearly four years, I felt that I had given research a more than fair chance to take hold of my heart. My heart would have none of it though, so I rationalized that my basic science background would offer me a better set of problem-solving skills. Hopefully these skills would allow me to do what I really wanted to do, which was to practice medicine.

That was going to be difficult if I couldn't get in to a medical school. Judging from the unpleasant look on my interviewer's face, I needed to start talking soon. So I launched into my best research presentation. After all my fumbling, expensive machine breakdowns, and some animal escapes, the research gods had taken pity on me. I at least had a decent amount of results to talk about. Finishing explaining my findings, I correlated them to human biology, development and disease processing, hopefully conveying to him that I had some understanding of the ultimate implications of my work. Lastly, I told him about my work's current directions and hinted at ideal outcomes and ambitious future medical applications. I could tell that the director was hooked and the clouds were clearing away from his forehead. My undergraduate institution was known for research, and I'm sure my school's legacy helped my story more than a little bit.

My luck was not to last though. The director next asked me how research fit into my plans for the future. Since they really did not, I told him the truth. I wanted to be a caring clinician first and family man, which is also…well… tied for first. My contribution to research would be along the lines of developing new techniques or translating basic science findings to the clinical realm. I could tell that the director, who had devoted decades of his life to basic research, viewed the pure clinician with a bit of contempt. This was clear when I was almost thrown out of my interview, which ended with a forceful, "do you even know about our research thesis?" After a morning of presentations, I obviously did, but that wasn't the point. Thus ended my misadventure for the day, and a few weeks later a thin envelope arrived.

Eventually things worked themselves out, and I entered medical school, despite my inability to tell people what they wanted to hear. It is important to maintain an open mind and explore new things, but eventually I had to be true to my personal convictions. If I disagree with a future interviewer about a strong belief, I hope that I will be able to tell them, and explain to them why.

--Char DeCroos

What Were They Thinking?

"What's the capital of Mozambique?" the interviewer asked me. A few seconds passed as I struggled to first understand the relevance of the question and then to respond with an appropriate answer. Up until that moment, I thought that my interview day at Duke had flowed quite smoothly. The interview process at Duke is all day and early in the morning, my host had shown me the admissions office where I dropped off my luggage. I had my picture taken for my ID badge and met my fellow interviewees. Following lunch and several presentations extolling the virtues of Duke Med, the time of reckoning had arrived. Looking around the waiting room, I could see that the other applicants probably felt as I felt; we were not a nervous group, for everyone had experienced a few chats with admissions personnel. The atmosphere was calm and cordial. People around me engaged in idle chit chat; the kind that no one remembers a few minutes later but at the moment seems to be the most engrossing and engaging conversation ever. I sat in my chair and read the ubiquitous information packets given at all interviews. The interviewer showed up a few minutes later. I was his first interviewee of the day, and he gripped my hand in a strong handshake. And so it began.

The first few questions centered on my family life and why I was subjecting myself to the arduous process of applying to medical school. The mood of the interview shifted quite dramatically when he asked, "So what can you tell me about oxygen free radicals?" I attempted to explain free radicals in terms of electron pairing. Still not understanding why I was being asked to explain biochemistry, I tried to lead the discussion towards my research in genetics, hoping to converse about scientific issues with which I was more familiar. The interviewer was not to be baited, and I soon found myself racking my brain for information about antioxidants and the foods that contain them. As a genetics major, he probably felt that I should be well versed in the nuances of free radical research; however, my answers portrayed my ignorance of the topic. If there had been a mirror in the interview room, I am almost certain that I would have seen the color drain from my face as my cheery disposition gave way to perplexed incredulity at the direction the interview was taking. I stumbled my way through questions about statistics and economics. I learned that I had no inkling of where the Santa Maria might be docked today or even if it still existed. My thoughts about the city of Baltimore were examined, and I was asked to describe my favorite place to live and why. For a while, I thought I could keep pace with the interviewer and somehow answer the questions in a vague manner that was mostly correct if I left out the details; the interviewer did not seem impressed. He soon resorted to factual questions such as when the Magna Carta was signed and the reaction products of complex organic chemistry synthesis equations to which I had to admit my lack of knowledge. Even questions to which I thought I had general answers, the interviewer would press, "Are you just guessing or do you know for certain?" In light of such scrutiny, I often resigned myself to saying, "I do not know the answer."

After what I perceived to be hours of random and frustrating questions, the interviewer ended by simply asking, "Do you have any questions for me?" My instinctive reaction was, "What was that all about?" but I did not pursue that line of questioning. Back in the waiting area, I sat in my chair thinking about the frustrating and terrible interview that I had just endured. My pondering was interrupted by a first-year medical student who walked into the waiting lounge and shared his interview experience with all who were present. I was surprised to hear him admit that he thought his interview at Duke was his worst one at any school. As I left the admissions office that day, I allowed myself to entertain the outlandish theory that if Duke looks for students who seem to interview terribly, then I must be guaranteed a place in the incoming class. Considering where I am today, I have realized that as an interviewee, I had no idea what the person across the table was thinking. Perhaps he wanted me accept the fact that I will not always have the answers to questions posed to me whether it be at a medical school interview or when a family member inquires about his or her loved one who is in the intensive care unit. He made me realize that it is all right to admit that you do not have all the answers as long as you are honest with yourself and others. Indeed, there have been many situations where I found myself out of my element, not knowing the answers immediately. Being true to myself, I did the work and sought out the answers, learning in the process that I am oftentimes my own worst critic. I have also discovered that the capital of Mozambique is Maputo.

--Gabriel Chong

The Interview Gone Bad

On November 4, 1999, I turned 21, and I was going to school at the University of Wisconsin-Madison. A week earlier, I had strained muscles in my back such that on my birthday, I was drugged up on muscle relaxants and could not drink much. The following year, I went easy on my birthday so that I could get up the next day and drive to St. Louis for my first medical school interview. The drive went well, and except for being locked out of the dorm for 20 minutes, everything on the fifth was great.

On the morning of November 6, 2000, I awoke in the cinder block cube that was my room, used the floor showers down the hall, donned the new suit and tie that I had bought the summer before, and I fastened my cuffs with new, monogrammed birthday cuff links. I went downstairs to the dining area and had breakfast with a kid I had met the night before, and really could not stand. At one point, he was milking a free breakfast from the SNMA people, whom he openly ridiculed when sitting next to me. As an aside, you will meet people like this on the interview trail, and yes, they will be accepted to schools and they will come to represent the medical profession.

It is hard to say exactly where the day turned for the worst, but we can start with the morning tour around the school and hospital. I wore a light wool suit, without an overcoat, because I could not afford one, and without an umbrella, because I saw no need to own one when wearing jeans to classes. But the rain began, and this outfit was a little different. On numerous occasions, people stopped me and told me to get out of the rain in a "nice suit like that."

After our grand tour, much of which was thankfully indoors, they took the group of interviewees upstairs to have lunch with medical students and medical school staff. I sat directly across the table from the dean of the school, who had just recently become best friends with one of my fellow interviewees. They had been discussing what would happen in Israel should Netenyahu return, and the interviewee's sister was actually in Israel studying at the time. People have great stories, and in the end, it is not that you have to make stories up for yourself; you just have to embellish those you already have. Don't miss out because you fail to adopt common practice.

Upon sitting down, I realized that all the men at the table had thrown their ties over their shoulders to eat. It was not something I had ever done before, but I decided to give it a shot. What I could not realize at the time was that my shoulders were wider than anyone else at the table, and my tie does not really stay put when I lean forward in the least. So sitting at lunch, in front of the dean of the medical school and his new advisor on Middle East relations, in my damp, pilled wool suit, I leaned forward and my tie fell flat onto my plate of food. I do not remember what we ate that day, but it was something creamy and with a decent smell. Not only did it get on my tie, I could smell lunch for the rest of the day.

After the meal, I had my interview with a doctor and I thought that this might turn things around. I arrived at his office five minutes early, not too early, and he was not there. It was not quite 1 p.m., so he could have been at lunch. His secretary of sorts said that she would call him and find out where he was, which turned out to be on the other side of Barnes-Jewish Hospital. So I took a seat while he walked back, via the admissions office to pick up my file, because it wasn't that he had forgotten that he had an interview that day—he had absolutely no idea that anyone was coming.

He made it back to his office at a quarter after the hour, had me wait outside for five more minutes while he looked over my file, and then he brought me in. The doctor had a second degree in biostatistics, and, rather than ask me any questions based on my file, he grilled me about changes in patient outcomes due to HMOs. After that, he asked me questions about the differences in Bush's and Gore's health care plans, and how those plans would alter the number of uninsured in the U.S.

This disaster was scheduled for one hour, just a bit shorter than the sinking of the Titanic, but 30 minutes in, his next appointment arrived—early. My interviewer kindly made him wait for a minute, and without sitting back down in his chair, told me why my application was not what it needed to be and that while I would not get into that medical school, if I hurried, I might be able to salvage a spot at another one.

I do not feel this is a representative example of how that university runs its medical school, but it is definitely my only experience with the institution. The point I was trying to make is that these disasters happen, and they can happen at the worst possible times on the trail—like when you are just starting out. In the end, I am of the mind that you cannot prepare for interviews, because you cannot prepare for interviewers; things will work out, even if it is not how you initially wanted them to; and you should not waste a good birthday night of drinking for one medical school interview.

--Jesse Waggoner

The Stress Test

Virtually every pre-medical student has heard the "urban myth" regarding the stress interview. Prospective student (let's call him Bob) enters the room, shakes hands, and the interview is begun. Halfway into Bob's heavily rehearsed "why I want to be a doctor" spiel, the interviewer comments: "It's rather warm in here, don't you think? Would you mind opening the window over there?" Poor, unknowing Bob heads over to said window and tries to open it, but the window will not budge. He tries again and again, pulling harder and harder, becoming visibly frustrated…for Bob is unaware that the window is fixed-nailed down to the frame, all so that the interviewer can see how Bob reacts under stress. And although this story will live forever in the minds of pre-medical and medical students alike, the stress interview rarely occurs in today's application process. But "rarely" is hardly solace for the unlucky individuals who do come across the stress interview—like myself.

My first medical school interview occurred at Stanford University. I had arrived promptly at 7:45 a.m. whereupon I was immediately escorted to my faculty interview. The interview began as I had expected; my assigned faculty member (let's call him Dr. Smith) asked me how I liked California, why I applied to Stanford in particular, and then proceeded to say: "So let's get to the question I have to ask or else I'll get booted off the admissions committee…why do you want to be a doctor?" Well-prepared for this question, I began to answer when three words into my speech, Dr. Smith picked up the phone and called his daughter. No "excuse me, I have to make a phone call," no "I'm sorry, but this is a really urgent matter…" In fact, Dr. Smith simply asked his daughter how she liked the warm weather they were having this week, if she enjoyed the steak dinner he cooked several nights ago, etc. And he spoke with her for a good 15 minutes, apparently unaware of the fact that I was sitting in the room, expecting an actual interview.

So what did I do? I simply looked around at the pictures on his desk, checked out the posters on the wall…visually scanning everything simply to keep myself calm. And really, I had no idea whether this type of behavior was standard in interviews or not, given that this was my first real interview ever. So finally, Dr. Smith ended the conversation with his daughter and simply stared at me for a while, whereupon I continued what I had been saying before he picked up the phone (as if the incident never even happened). Assuming that the rest of the interview would be more according to my expectations, we moved on, and Dr. Smith began asking me about my research. When I brushed upon an experimental tool we had used known as the Morris water maze (essentially a mini-pool for rodents with a platform submerged in the water, it typically tests learning behavior and memory, but can also be simply used as a stressor-how appropriate!), he stopped me. "Stand up and show me how big such a maze really is…and then go ahead and show me what a rat would look like doing such a test." So I proceeded to do all this, but could not given how cramped his office was, and simply tried to verbally explain what it would be like if I were a four-legged rodent rather than an extremely baffled medical school interviewee. Finally, the interview came to a close, he told me how wonderful his previous applicant was and how she was definitely going to be accepted into the school and escorted me out of the office. Perfect ending, right? After that, I spent the next two hours simply sitting outside, recovering from whatever had happened, trying to convince myself that not all my interviews were going to be like this.

Honestly, I have no idea what Dr. Smith was looking for when he interviewed me, but apparently he liked what he saw because I was accepted into the school very shortly thereafter. All that I know is that I stayed calm throughout the entire fiasco. I never took any of his behavior personally and ultimately the interview remained more like a conversation (albeit an extremely bizarre one) throughout its entirety. And that's really how all medical interviews should be—a conversation—for virtually every other interviewer I had would talk just as much, if not more, than me. So the only advice I can give applies to all interviews in general. Remain calm, open-minded and light-hearted and you'll do just fine. And interviews are going to be highly spontaneous (especially the stress interview), so although it is beneficial to have some idea of what may be asked and how you might respond, never simply spit out a rehearsed speech word for word. Interviewers will see right through that…no matter their methods.

--Nancy Edwards

Staying True

I am very happy that I got into medical school at all. The total count of schools I applied to was 13 and the number of interviews I obtained was six. That's right: less than half the schools I applied to wanted to see my ugly mug. Of those six, two schools waitlisted me, two schools rejected me and two schools accepted me. The last interview I had was at Duke.

How this system works: it's completely unpredictable. This process is so competitive that the selection criterions become inane after a while, so that breathing the wrong way will elicit an instant rejection. So the key to success in the interview process is being yourself. Trying very hard to please someone else by being something that you are not is very difficult and stressful; also, it may come off the wrong way to others, as I found out first-hand.

I think the reason why my Duke interview went so well was because at that point, I simply didn't care anymore. You will know what I am talking about when you have interview after interview in a short span of time. After a while, with all of the traveling and touring, the process becomes so repetitive that the schools blur together. I had reached this point by the time I hit Durham. Rejection letter after rejection letter was pouring in and I figured that Duke was an unattainable dream to someone like me. Sure I was pretty smart, but I wasn't looking at a 4.0 GPA and a 43 on the MCAT, so I just said "To hell with it...I'm only going to say what I feel, not what they want to hear." And I did just that. This demonstrated two things: who I was, and confidence in that respect. These things may not seem that important with all of the crazy hype that you hear about grades, MCAT scores, research and recommendations, but they are. It shows character, because no one wants robots for doctors anymore, they want people with history and depth. Whatever grades you pulled and whatever IQ you think you have, there are at least 50 other people out there who are better in that respect, but there is only ONE of you. Show these people who you are at the interview.

This brings me to my second point: rejection doesn't mean you are stupid and unqualified (UCSD made sure to tell me this in a very long rejection letter). What it means is that the medical school had someone in mind BEFORE they saw you and you weren't it when you arrived. If you are yourself when you enter and exit each interview, then you will be selected based upon that merit and not the other guy you were trying to be. Why go to a school that didn't want YOU?

Duke has two interviews, which is fairly typical, and each lasts about 30 minutes. My first interview went fine, but I thought that the second interview did not go so well after the interviewer asked me: "Name for me all the cytochromes on the electron transport chain of the mitochondria." Do you know what I did? I looked that guy right in the eye and said, "I really have no idea." I think this demonstrates an important lesson: be honest, with yourself and others. People respect this. No one wants a doctor who, when he doesn't know the answer, makes one up so that he won't look "stupid." Every doctor I have ever talked to hates precisely this attitude, because they discovered long ago that no one is perfect, that you can't know all the answers. So when you walk into the room: take a deep breath, smile and be yourself. The rest will happen automatically.

--Neil Hanson

Common Interview Questions

You've already read about the horror stories out there about hapless interviewees and the wicked curveballs they were thrown, but it's important to realize that the majority of interviews are simply conversations in which the school tries to get a sense of who you really are. They are not out to get you.

Even so, you might ask if there's anything you can do to prepare for the interview day, The answer is plenty. One of the most important things you can do is to have a deep and honest understanding of yourself. This is what medical schools seek from you during the interview, and it's critical to have given thought about it beforehand. To aid you in this end, a list of questions is included below. Realize that these are questions commonly asked in medical school interviews, but that you should not use them to formulate a scripted answer you can spit back during the big day. You'll likely sound like a robot and won't be applauded for your memorization skills (although they will come in handy during gross anatomy). Instead, these questions should guide you in knowing yourself better. This is essential since you won't be capable of anticipating every possible question that can be asked of you during the interview day. With a good understanding of what you're about, though, you can answer questions with confidence and ace those interviews.

Personal

Tell me about yourself.

Who are you?

What three adjectives would best describe you?

Tell me about your family.

Who are your heroes?

What's your favorite film/book/song?

What do you do for fun?

> *NOTE: Don't get too crazy. For example, going to bars with friends is not the best thing to mention here.*

Tell me about your hobbies.

What motivates you?

What are you most proud of? Least proud of?

What do you perceive your strengths to be? Weaknesses?

NOTE: It's always good to try turning a weakness into a strength. For example, I overextend myself at times, and get too involved. But this has definitely helped me learn how to manage my time better.

What volunteer work have you done?

Academics

What was your favorite course in college? Least favorite?

Which instructor made the greatest impact on you? Why?

Tell me about your research.

NOTE: Know your research well! This is crucial. Nothing makes a worse impression than not knowing the details or your work and its applications. You should be the expert!

Why did you choose the undergraduate institution you did?

What achievement are you most proud of?

If you could do college all over again, what would you do differently?

Motivations

What type of medical practice are you interested in (e.g., private, academic, rural-based)?

NOTE: It is completely acceptable to say you don't know. You are not expected to know this at this point in your career. But it would be nice to discuss some possible interests.

What specialty appeals to you most? Why?

Why do you want to go to our medical school? What do you think it offers? How can you contribute to next year's class?

NOTE: Do yourself a favor and look up information on the school the day before your visit. If your school has an interested curriculum or volunteer activities that they talk about on their web site, it might be worth asking about it.

If you could stand before the admissions committee right now, what would you say?

Why should we admit you?

What other schools are you applying to?

If you don't get into medical school, what would you do instead?

If you never became a doctor, what profession would you choose?

Where do you see yourself in five years? 10? 20?

Healthcare

Where do you see the state of healthcare going in the next 20 years?

What do you think of socialized medicine?

What do you think is the biggest problem with the U.S. healthcare system? How would you fix it?

What is your conception of the ideal physician?

What aspects of being a doctor appeal to you most? Least?

Ethics

Tell me your views on abortion.

What do you think of embryonic stem cell research?

> *NOTE: Most people in large academic centers see the advantages, rather than the ethical holdups, of stem cell research.*

Do you believe human cloning beneficial or harmful to mankind? Why?

Do you think healthcare is a right or a privilege?

> *NOTE: Saying it's a privilege will usually get you weird looks.*

Should a person be allowed to sell their kidney?

What do you think of passive euthanasia? Active euthanasia?

The off-beat (not frequently asked, but good to give a thought to nonetheless)

If you were a fruit, what fruit would you be? Why?

What animal characterizes you best?

If you went back in time, what event would you change?

What TV show would you like to be on?

If you could have dinner with three people, past or present, who would they be? What would you serve?

If you were stranded on a desert island for life, what three possessions would wish to have?

What was your most embarrassing moment?

If you won a million dollars, what would you do with the money?

What will the epitaph on your grave read?

If you had to cut off a finger to get into medical school, would you do it?

--*Yolanda Chik*

An Interview with Brenda Armstrong, Director of Admissions, Duke Medical School

"Wouldn't you like to know?"

Every pre-med wants the inside scoop on how to conquer the application process. I know what you're thinking: "Who would know more about the application process than the Director of Admissions?" We all know the answer...no one! This is why we asked the Director of Admissions at Duke, Dr. Brenda Armstrong, about her candid feelings on questions that undergraduates are dying to know. Not only was this interview informative, some of the answers may surprise you.

What's the most common misconception about the medical school admissions process?

Armstrong: The most common misconception is that all you need is high grades and high MCAT scores to get into medical school. Most people come in thinking that they don't have to do the other pieces: that they're not expected to have done a fair amount of community service and volunteerism. Extracurricular leadership on campus is just as important to us as grades and MCATs.

How important are extracurricular activities as opposed to GPA and MCAT scores?

Armstrong: It varies from school to school but at Duke we weigh these activities the same as grades and MCAT scores. It's one of multiple parameters that we look at when we start evaluating an applicant.

How vital is research during undergrad?

Armstrong: If you are applying for an MD/PhD program, it's absolutely essential. Outside of that, you really ought to do it because you're interested in it and not because you think it will look good on your transcript. Some of it depends on the type of school you are applying to. If you are applying to a research institution it will carry some value. If you are applying to a school that is known for clinical practice, it won't be as important.

How has the admissions process changed over the last few years?

Armstrong: I think people are finally realizing that MCATs and grade point averages don't predict who will be a good doctor. It doesn't even predict who is going to be a good researcher. There are other things that are equally important that tell you about whether someone will be successful as a medical student. A great deal of it has to do with building a total picture of an applicant: looking at what their educational and personal experiences have been, whether they have had obstacles to overcome, whether they have had incredible advantages that they have used to do something with, whether they've had an investment in people, whether or not they took the time to see part of life that is different from there own so that they would appreciate it and treat it with respect and dignity if they saw it again as medical students and physicians. All of those things are very important and they are just as important as how you study for a chemistry exam or how well you prepared for the MCAT.

Does the choice of major or double majoring affect the admissions decision?

Armstrong: No…that's easy. Not only does the choice of major not have a real significant impact, whether you decide to major in two different areas does not have an impact either.

How should students use medical school rankings when deciding on schools?

Armstrong: They shouldn't. It's unfortunate that so many people put too much emphasis on these rankings that are arbitrary. They really do not measure an institution for anything more than how many research dollars they bring in and some index of how "smart the schools are" and those indices are usually MCATs and average GPAs. We all know that there are huge fallacies in trusting that and nothing else. I'm saying that coming from Duke where Duke ends up in the Top Six of these rankings every year, but if people are coming to Duke because of this they will be sorely disappointed.

What advice would you give to undergraduates who want to apply to medical school?

Armstrong: They have to realize that the process of applying to medical school starts in the first year and they should see it as a four-year process. They should seek out good advice and find out who their pre-med advisors are and identify themselves early as being pre-med. They should not only take the prerequisites but take difficult courses in everything, not just science. Take difficult courses in the things that they are interested in, their majors, which may be in humanities. They should also take the time to explore a diversity of classes because it will be the last time they will be able to do that. They have to time manage very well in undergraduate school in order to be able to not only put appropriate priorities to their academics but also to have time to do something else. I would encourage students to really take the time to see medicine up close so they can decide whether or not medicine is something they really want to do.

Does it look bad to take the MCAT more than once? What if you do worse the second or third time around?

Armstrong: Most schools will take the best scores, first of all. There is a great deal of data that suggests that after two times it becomes diminishing returns in that you really don't see that much of a change.

Does one bad grade ruin an applicant's chance?

Armstrong: No. Most of us look at grades like trends. We look at the bottom line but then we look at how you got to the bottom line. We want to make sure of what happened to make you have a bad grade. If things started out bad and you worked your way through, statistical analysis will tell you that if you had a really bad semester it takes you awhile to overcome it. Instead of just looking at the bottom line we also look at trends.

What is the one thing that you always wanted to tell pre-meds but never got the chance to say?

Armstrong: I think the one thing that I'm so impressed about is the fact that they obsess so much at the interview and they seem so unnatural at the interview because of it. Usually I always try to tell them that no one is out to get them and that the interview day, for instance here at Duke, we try to make it a comfortable day. We try to have people that will ask questions in a respectful and inquiring way without threatening or demeaning the students. We also try to give them lots of opportunity to meet students who are the only persons who can really reassure the prospective students that they won't get eaten alive once they get here. I think of all the things I want to tell them, the top one is when they get to the interview piece of it, they really ought to relax and enjoy the day and come with an agenda to find out more about the school.

Does it look bad to take science courses away from your undergraduate institution?

Armstrong: It looks bad to take your pre-medical prerequisites away. You do not ever want to do that. You can take other courses that are not required but you do not want to take prerequisites anywhere other than your base school.

Scientific versus non-scientific summer programs. Does it matter?

Armstrong: I think everybody should do something related to science or health at least one summer. Whether it is research, a summer program, a shadowing or volunteering experience, I think at least one of the three summers for traditional students ought to be that kind of context.

Does it matter which medical school you attend when it comes to internship and residency positions in the future?

Armstrong: That's difficult. The real answer is that good students are everywhere. Whether you went to a "top tier school" or not, good students are everywhere. The politics of the residency match have a handicap that favors students who go to elite schools. No one will say that or stand up and say it. Truth of the matter is that if you're a good student at an elite school, it makes it easier for you as you start to look, especially among very competitive residencies. We're finding now that we have more slots than we can even fill. If you go to medical school and do well, you will stand out and people will notice that in the process. It's just that you end up having to have a set of cheerleaders at the school that is not quite so well known and you might not need that if you are coming out of a school that is very well known or thought to be a "top tier school."

Older versus younger applicants. Pros and cons.

Armstrong: Older applicants bring a perspective of maturity that is very settling. I think the nice thing in our classes is that older students are able to put things in perspective a lot better because they have seen a little more of life. An exam does not carry the same angst for them that it will carry for a student coming right out of college. The younger students have an enthusiasm and sort of naivety about medicine that is really refreshing. Having a mix of both in the class is nice.

Do you need any clinical experience to be considered for medical school?

Armstrong: You have to some clinical experience. Even students who have limited time and focus more on research and want to get into MD/PhD programs are expected to have some clinical exposure.

Do admissions committees look down on taking a year off before starting medical school?

Armstrong: No. In fact we are encouraging students to do more of that because it gives students independence and maturity and we don't care what they do during that year. Most students feel they have to do an internship or something else. They don't have to do anything: they just have to be able to say "I took a year off because I needed a break before I started these intense eight or more years." We want people to come to medical school when they are ready.

Last question: what factors go into putting a class of 100 together?

Armstrong: That's the toughest question. We try to think about people who have a number of different talents. We want people who are interested in research because this is a research institution. We want people who are interested in learning how to take care of patients and then developing newer ways of taking care of patients. We want people who might end up in research but don't want to go the MD/PhD route. We want people who are thinking about better ways to deliver health care and new policies for healthcare. We want women and minorities. We want the faces in our classes to look like the communities that they will go out and serve. By doing it that way, the people in our classes learn the kind of respect for patients by learning to respect their classmates and their gifts. As a result, they are much more powerfully equipped to do culturally competent care when their class is culturally competent. Those are the things that we look at.

--Kara King

Financial Aid and Scholarships

CHAPTER 8

Applications and Interviews

Applying to medical schools can be a costly endeavor; therefore, you should start planning early. Even before you start considering the cost of medical school, itself!

Designate an amount of money that you can afford to put aside for the application process and interviews. If you're planning on applying to a ton of schools, particularly those outside of your state and a plane's ride away, $2,000 is not an unreasonable amount. Your personal budget will influence how many schools you apply to, the geographical distribution of the schools and where you will actually go for an interview. Once you have a good estimate of how much money you have, then investigate the schools to which you decide to apply. For example, if you decide to apply to state schools outside of your state of residency, find out if those state schools have very strict residency policies. Before you send them your money, check to make sure that their requirements do not include residency in that state!

One of the first financial decisions you make is whether you are going to take an MCAT review course. Many review courses can be quite expensive (usually over $1,500).

To help you with the actual MCAT registration fee of $210, there is a Financial Assistance Program (FAP) that is intended to help students in severe financial need. You can apply for the FAP at the AAMC web site. The process is extremely short, but you must have your own and your parents' tax return information close by. You will be required to submit your parents' tax information even if your parents do not help support you anymore; therefore, even if you are no longer a dependent, you will still have to provide your parents' information. If your FAP application is approved, your MCAT registration fee will be reduced to $85 and you will have the right to send the AMCAS application to 11 schools for free. For any additional schools, you will have to pay $30 per school. Without this program, it costs $160 for the processing your application and sending it to one school, and $30 for each additional school, so depending on how many schools you apply to, the FAP could save you between $500 and $600. In addition, a lot of schools will waive the application fee for the secondary application once you have been approved for the FAP. Some schools explicitly state this in the instructions that come with the secondary application. Other schools will give you the same benefits only after you call and inquire directly. AMCAS does not inform schools of your status directly. In most cases, the schools will simply ask you to attach a copy of your FAP approval letter to your application. The deadlines for the FAP are early, but even if you miss the deadline for the MCAT, you should still apply because you can still qualify for the application benefits.

The money you save on the MCAT and primary AAMC application will come in handy once the secondary applications start coming. Some secondary application fees can be quite expensive—up to $100. If your budget is limited, this is the time to think about crossing out some schools. When filling out the secondary applications you should be more selective than when you sent out your primary application. I did not follow up on all the secondary applications that I received. I sat down and thought about whether I would really go to such and such school if I were accepted. If the answer was no, instead of sending back the secondary application, I sent back a "Thank you, but…" letter. This is not completely necessary, since most schools will know you are not interested when they don't receive your secondary, but I think it's courteous. I also recommend that you weigh the significance of the fact that you received the secondary application from a certain school. Some schools send secondary applications to all of their applicants, while others send them to a certain percentage of the students whose applications they received, and a few schools send secondary applications only to students that they intend to interview. It all depends on how their director of admissions wants to run the show. Therefore, not every secondary application carries the same weight. But remember, you must fill out a secondary in order to have a chance at the next step—getting an interview.

Finally, if you are a procrastinator like I am, I suggest you get to know your postal system. Find out which post offices are open late. An airport will usually have a post office nearby that has the longest hours of operation. Inquire in advance about the quickest ways to get your finished application to a desired location by the designated deadline. USPS.com is a great way to figure out how much it will cost to send your application across the country overnight, in case you need it. I became a regular at my post office and I even got to know my mailman rather well during the months of anxious waiting.

--Ivana Nikolic

Financial Planning

Despite what the numbers seem to suggest, the goal of going to medical school is not to become as poor as possible. Tuition costs, even at state schools, can result in massive, seemingly prohibitive debt loads. Imagining how you will be able to pay back $150,000 when you are just out of school can be difficult for many students. The good news is that with careful planning, the debt accrual does not have to be staggering and you can "enjoy" your time in medical school. Here is how I conducted my search for the best, and yet affordable, medical education I could find

Several points to consider at the beginning:

- Develop a realistic picture of your current financial picture, including COMPREHENSIVE debt (car and insurance payments, ALL credit card bills, undergraduate loans left to be paid, any other debts to family or friends that require repayment on a timeline).
- Gather detailed information about your debts, such as interest rates, minimum payments due, maximal length of repayment time, whether or not consolidation is a wise option, whether being in medical school will postpone your repayment schedule and whether attending medical school will result in an interest rate reduction or decrease of loan amounts. There are some state programs in specific medical fields that will pay back your educational loans in proportion to the time you work in the state much like the armed services educational loan repayment plans. You will have to research the specifics related to your medical field of choice.
- Research health insurance options including whether or not you can remain on your parents' plan and, if not, whether your potential school will provide an affordable plan for you.
- Feel out your family for levels of financial support that may be available to you while you are in school. For example, will your older sibling (who earns a lot as a stockbroker) be able to help you out if your car unexpectedly breaks down? Will your parents be willing to co-sign your loans if necessary?

Once armed with this information about your financial state, you can begin to evaluate the financial picture of each school that you are considering. Here are some points to think about when considering the school:

- What is the basic cost per year? Make sure the book you are using is not a few years old or you may grossly underestimate this. The best source is obviously the financial aid offices of the schools.

- Are there any grants available from the school directly? How big are they? Do you have to apply for them or are you automatically considered? This varies widely amongst schools based on whether they are private or public and how big their endowment is. Some schools offer no grants, while others have generous ones that may cover more than half of the tuition costs.

- Are there specific scholarships available for areas you may be interested in studying? Ask how many current students receive inside/outside scholarships.

- Are there any special time periods for which you can be externally funded to reduce your overall debt load? For example, here at Duke, most students get grants from institutions such as the National Institutes of Health, the Howard Hughes Medical Institute or the Sarnoff Endowment which fund their third year of basic science research. Each student must individually find a mentor and submit a grant proposal to each institution to be considered for funding. Information about available grants is offered by our student affairs office during our second year.

- What types of loans are available at each school? In general, federally subsidized loans have the lowest interest rates and longest/most flexible repayment periods. If you are eligible for federal loans, you will have to apply for them each year that you are in school. There are also other private loan programs such as Medloans for both students and parents which are tailored to medical education. Lastly, some schools offer their own institutional loans which come directly from the school. The financial aid office of each school can provide details regarding what loan programs are available and how to apply for them.

- What is the local cost of living in the area of the school you are considering? Be realistic here and include rent, utilities, entertainment, food, etc. in your approximate numbers. One easy way to get an idea of what this will be is to track your spending for a few months before deciding on a school. Just total up how much you spend every month from your checking account and add what your expected rent and utilities would be wherever the school is located. If you do not use realistic figures, you will run out of money during the year. Obviously, it is usually more expensive to live in a major city than to live in a small town because of higher rent, eating and entertainment costs. Book and equipment costs are also something to consider if you are the type of person who buys every suggested textbook. These expenses add up quickly in medical school. Travel costs should also be included in this estimate if your family or significant other is far away from your school of choice. Lastly, consider whether you want to have a roommate.

Once you have financially evaluated all the schools at which you have interviews, just relax and enjoy the interviews. Use the interview day to decide what you like about the school, and ask any financial questions you have up front. After interviewing, I made a financial list for each school and a "what I like about it" list. I then compared the two lists to determine where I could get the best education in my field of interest for the least amount of money. Remember that intangibles, such as how much you like a place, should also weigh into your decision. You will spend four years in that location, so you should be able to enjoy the place and the people. If you decide that you want to attend a more expensive school for specific career reasons, you can use all the information you have gathered to plan for debt accrual and management. If you have two schools about which you feel similarly, then choose the one where you will have the lowest debt with the best terms of repayment.

I chose Duke because it has a unique curriculum, a strong academic tradition and it offered the best financial package of all the schools I considered. I worked for five years in between undergrad and medical school, so had paid off many previous debts. I can defer payment on the remaining loans until graduation. This area is very affordable and I expect my total loan accrual to be near the national average when I finish.

To sum it all up, there is a lot to consider when it comes to finances. Remember to pay attention to the details regarding future expenses. You will be more prepared and better off if you do.

--Kelley Hutcheson

Big Numbers

Yes, numbers DO exist with that many zeros attached to the end. Of course it took the signing of my loan papers for me to acknowledge the existence of such vast sums of money in the real world and not just in reference to some obscure formula we had to memorize for the MCAT. So, is it worth it to be in debt an amount equivalent to Avogadro's number upon graduation from medical school? How much impact should financial concerns have on your choice of a school?

The most pragmatic advice I have ever been given in regards to successful financial management is almost absurdly simple, as the best advice tends to be. Moreover, in keeping with the tradition of the best advice, this pearl of pecuniary wisdom is equally difficult, if not impossible, to consistently follow. Spend less than you earn. The economics are simple; avoiding debt is inarguably the most foolproof way to ensure financial security. Hence my first piece of advice:

Do your research

Find out what you would have to pay to attend your top choices—note that this task entails more than just comparing tuition costs from your laminated pocket copy of *U.S. News and World Report*'s exposé on medical schools. Find out what the average student actually pays after grants, scholarships and other forms of financial aid. You may find that some schools, whose listed tuition could buy you multiple luxury vehicles, are in fact more affordable than other seemingly less-pricey schools. Also, keep your eyes out for outside scholarships. Though not as numerous as those for undergrad, they do exist. Start by searching online; there is a vast amount of financial aid information available on the Web. Investigate scholarships from outside sources such as: unions to which your parents belong, local churches, civic organizations and National Medical Fellowships for minority students. Find out how close you can come to adhering to the paradigm of spending less than you earn. Since the amount of bacon you'll be bringing home during your medical training will not likely threaten the world's swine population, this means avoiding debt will require cautious spending.

So, why did I turn down a free education at a good school for a considerably less-than-free education at an excellent school? Thus begins the part of my diatribe where I offer a loophole to the difficult (albeit indubitably sound) advice dispensed above:

Debt, if necessary, is best incurred for something that will appreciate in value

Why do you think banks are so eager to loan money to future MDs? Your medical education is an investment, one with a well-documented rate of return, whose value does not immediately depreciate when you drive it off the lot. It is no secret that incomes rise exponentially as high school, college and graduate school degrees are earned. You are preparing to enter a field with incredible job security and historically reasonable reimbursement. The money you spend obtaining a degree in medicine is a small sacrifice now for what will ultimately be a very rewarding (financially and otherwise) lifelong career.

At the end of the day, you have to follow your heart

As mushy as this may sound, this decision determines where you will be spending the next four years of your life. Sure, you'll probably spend some weekends memorizing more biochemical pathways than phone numbers, but you will also make some really great friends, do some really amazing stuff and learn more about yourself and those things that truly define your character than can ever be gleaned from your anatomy atlas or pathology textbook. So, if you find yourself drawn toward one school with an inexplicable sense of peace, contentment and excitement for its people, program and atmosphere, I suggest that you trust that intuition. This abstraction completely contradicts the systematic, concrete nature to which we as scientists historically cling, but where would science be without instinct?

--Lauren Parks

Decisions, Decisions, Decisions

When I first read the tuition prices of medical schools as a prospective medical student, I did not even know how to start thinking about it. The combination of tuition and living expenses was so much more money than I had ever dealt with. The concept of spending all that money for four years was rather numbing, especially since many of my friends were receiving fantastic job offers from consulting and engineering firms.

I knew from the beginning that financial aid was going to be an important part of my medical school decision. Neither I, nor my parents, had the money to pay for my medical education. However, another factor that weighed heavily on me was my career goals as a physician. I have always wanted to work in underserved populations—both in the U.S. and in Third World countries. I dream of participating in a program like Doctors without Borders. With these dreams, however, comes an added realization: I probably will not have a high-paying career in which it is relatively easy to pay off loans I acquire.

But I do not want my financial decisions now to substantially restrict my career options in the future.

With all of these thoughts in mind, I began to go through the process of applying for financial aid in January. The first step is getting your taxes (and your parents' taxes) done. This makes the process of filling out the FAFSA and any other applications, such as Need Access, much easier. The FAFSA is the Free Application for Federal Student Aid; Need Access is an example of a supplementary application that some schools require to get even more financial information. I was lucky because my parents and I had been filing the FAFSA for years to apply for financial aid at my private high school and in college, so we worked together to get the necessary information and file the form. I had the information sent to all the schools that I had applied to, even the ones I had not heard from yet. Then I began the process of waiting. However, do not forget to make sure that your financial aid application is progressing. Call your schools to make sure they have gotten all the information. Forms get lost all the time. It happened to me, but the situation was easily remedied by staying on top of things. You do not want to lose out on aid because of mislaid forms!

By March or April I had received my acceptance letters, and the financial aid offers started to trickle in. I found that I had to call financial aid offices regularly to find out when I would be receiving the offers. How can you make a decision without information from all the schools? In some cases, this is inevitable. One of my state schools did not process financial aid information for first-year medical students until June! I found that extremely frustrating when I was trying to make an informed decision. You might think that all your difficulties are over once you have the offers. While that is true, I agonized over the final decision. Comparing offers between different schools can be practically impossible. How do you compare a school with fewer grants but more subsidized loans with a school with more grants and far less subsidized loans? All schools have different tuitions and living expenses. Some are calculated on 12 month years, others on 10 or even 13 month years. In addition, of course, living expenses vary considerably. The process can be overwhelming. My parents and I spent hours, individually and on the phone, attempting to compare my offers. In the end, even when I thought I knew what the best offer was, it was only part of my final decision. I did not think an out-of-state state school was the best choice for me academically, despite their generous financial offer of in-state tuition. Also, living at home in Oregon would have saved me money, but it was not ideal for both academic and personal reasons.

As May 15th and the inevitable decision date approached, I was seriously considering four schools: Duke, Oregon Health and Science University, University of Texas Southwestern and Vanderbilt. When I finally made my decision, I chose to attend Duke. Duke was neither my cheapest nor most expensive option. Nevertheless, medical school is four years of a lot of hard work and I wanted to be a student somewhere I thought I would have a life. When I made my final choice, the "happiness quotient" mostly outweighed the financial aspects of the decision.

--Meghan Liel

Choosing a Medical School

CHAPTER 9

Now that you've applied and been accepted to some medical schools, which one do you choose? Although the decision is one you'll have to make on your own, there questions that every prospective med student must ask and factors that he must weigh. This chapter will discuss the choices that will affect each and every med school decision.

Practical Tips for Choosing a Medical School

Use the application process as an opportunity to narrow down and rank your schools

Don't worry about being disappointed if you don't get into the school you ranked number one or two. But be prepared to be flexible, which will be easy as long as you avoid applying to places where you would not see yourself being happy. Your own contentment in your medical school environment has a lot to do with your success; you're clearly already smart, so, in addition to the resources of the school, your overall happiness there and the people around you will make a big difference in the success of your medical school career. Doing a lot of research about where you want to go while applying not only helps you later during the choice process, but it also improves the quality of your applications and interviews dramatically, and may even give you a great deal of self-insight.

Get applications done early

Don't put it off, and don't by shy with recommenders or pre-medical advisors about politely reminding them to get materials in on time. Also fill out your financial aid forms early. This will give you earlier acceptance AND financial aid award offers, thereby giving you more time to think through the realistic parameters of your options.

Come to understand the different residency and sub-specialty training pathways

Before and during the application process. Also investigate what the different career paths of a physician can look like, before applying to medical schools. Having an idea of the two or three paths you might take will help guide you to apply to a group of schools that will be a good fit.

Try to imagine yourself at different places

What would you do in your spare time, walk or drive to the hospital? Run in a forest or workout in a city gym? Make dinner at home or eat at a restaurant? Go out to a college pub with friends or dance at city nightclub? Visit with your family or take a trip with your friends? And, how many of these things would you actually have time for, relative to particular curriculums at different schools? Make an actual list of pros and cons.

Don't ignore your gut reaction

If you're down to two schools or locations, flip a coin: heads for Boston and tails for Los Angeles. If you wince when LA comes up on top, maybe you shouldn't go there, or at least you should re-evaluate the short-term and long-term benefits more carefully.

Don't use the revisit weekend as a primary decision driver

It should only be used as the sanity check. This brief exposure can be helpful, but it can also be misleading; the weather could be an anomaly that weekend, students are encouraged to be extra nice and events are planned that may not represent the normal daily life of a place. At the end of the day, the vigor of the admissions office at putting together a good revisit weekend may not correlate to actual life at that medical school, and quality of the curriculum.

Anticipate that you will go through an adjustment period at your new medical school

This will probably have more to do with the nature of medical school, rather than your choice of medical school. This may be a greater adjustment when you have taken time off from school, or are moving to a new type of environment and away from loved ones. It's okay to struggle with this transition a bit. Let it force you to discover and enjoy your surroundings fully, engage in participating in and improving the community around you, and find your own path.

--Jason Langheier

The Deal Breakers

Choosing a medical school is obviously a very personal, individual decision. However, it's also clear that the majority of applicants tend to heavily weigh a few specific traits in this process. Namely, one typically chooses a school based on some individual balancing of considerations regarding (in alphabetical order):

- Curriculum
- Finances
- Location
- Personal Reasons
- Reputation

Here's a brief exploration of some things to keep in mind regarding these five categories:

Curriculum

For some, curriculum is THE definitive factor, as it tends to be a major variable among different schools. Unfortunately, a school's style is often not easy to ascertain, especially before you have the chance to visit. That said, a few dominant schools of thought have emerged, and upon visiting schools it can quickly become clear which methodology a particular school espouses. First, there is the traditional approach. Typically such a curriculum is largely lecture-based, and composed of a number of separate courses in various disciplines. For example, during the first few months of the year one might study basic science, like genetics and biochemistry, and have exams in each of these courses, which exist at entirely separate entities with separate grades, professors, etc. Later on in the year one might take courses in anatomy, physiology, etc., and again, exams and laboratory exercises would likely be separate, although clinical experiences and a limited amount of small group work is often incorporated.

On the other hand, a growing number of schools employ newer, "non-traditional" techniques, like problem-based learning (PBL). As the amount of lecture time is being decreased at many schools across the country, PBL has emerged as a more dominant, in-vogue methodology. In such a curriculum, lecture hours are typically minimized, or somehow diminished compared to those at a more traditional school, so as to accommodate group exercises. In these exercises, one is given a case study or specific assignment, which is subsequently discussed in small groups, typically facilitated by a clinician or other faculty member(s). Work is divided amongst participants, research is done at home, and subsequent presentations to the group may occur, followed by discussions. This is a relatively new initiative in medical education, having emerged more prominently over the past few decades. Its rationale is predicated upon the notion that group learning is more "active" learning, and that active learning tends to impart more longevity. As the amount of medical knowledge continues to escalate, schools have come to recognize that students cannot possibly learn everything about medicine in four years. Instead, curricular innovations like PBL aim to prepare students to be "lifelong learners," able to stay up-to-date in the rapidly changing field of medicine.

Clearly, there are positives and negatives to the various educational methodologies, and often what is a positive feature for some may be a drawback for others. In addition, while some schools employ a mixture of these different methodologies, a general philosophy is often evident. For example, Duke is known for being very non-traditional in its overall style, and is quite unique in placing students on the hospital wards full-time during the second year, rather than waiting until the third year as most schools do. Only a handful of other schools endorse this practice, including the University of Pennsylvania and Baylor College of Medicine. With these differences in mind, it is particularly important to ascertain what style might work best FOR YOU, to help you make an informed choice about which school best fits your preferences. Although some worry about board scores, residency match statistics, etc., it's probably not a good idea for you to attend a school that uses a group learning style when you know you're more of a didactic or individual learner, for example. Examine the particular web sites of each school, which typically contain curricular information, as well as discussion-based web sites like the Student Doctor Network (www.studentdoctor.net). The AAMC also compiles a "curriculum directory," which aims to detail the courses, grading philosophy and other important aspects of each school, although it remains incomplete (http://services.aamc.org/currdir/start.cfm). In many cases, you may not be able to ascertain the curricular style of a school until you have the opportunity to interview there and speak to current students. This is often the best way to get a feel for what life is really like at a particular school, and whether or not it suits your learning style. School web sites may also be helpful, many of which are easily reached via this web site: http://www.aamc.org/ students/applying/admissions.htm.

Some students find themselves confused about what style they prefer, and that's okay. For some, curriculum is not a critical factor in choosing a school, perhaps because both learning styles are amiable, or because other factors are much more important to them. Consider the following questions to help you ascertain which style best suits you.

First, think back to those lecture-based classes you had as an undergraduate.

- What was good about this style?
- What was bad?
- Did you attend class, or prefer to learn by reading on your own, at home or in the library?
- Do you need the pressure of an upcoming exam to really get motivated, or do you read throughout the semester?

Next, compare and contrast this experience with that of the small seminars you might have taken.

- What was good about this style?
- What was bad?
- Did you benefit from more active participation?
- Was learning more, or less efficient?
- Was learning more, or less enjoyable?

Now think about small group projects you may have done.

- Did you thrive in this setting, or dread having to be so dependent on others?
- Were you frustrated at the lack of preparation from other students, or did you thrive in this environment?
- Did you find many projects or small group exercises to be valuable, or a waste of time?

Finally, consider some of your favorite classes, and ponder what made them special or educationally valuable.

Contemplating these factors may help you recognize an underlying curricular preference. And, as always, talk to students! No one knows what a school is like better than the students who live through it every day!

Finances

When faced with the difficult decision of choosing which school to attend, it's hard for money not to enter into the equation. In particular, financial aid packages can become an enormous headache, for it's not at all uncommon for a student to be offered little aid at their top choice school, whereas other institutions may offer substantial grant money, loans or even scholarships. And tuition at state schools is typically significantly lower than at private schools. What should you do if your first choice is a private school that costs

$50,000 per year, whereas your state school would only be around $5,000 per year?

There are two basic schools of thought on this issue. Some hold that it is preferable to minimize the amount of money one borrows or has to pay to attend medical school, since it becomes difficult to pay off the loans once deferment periods end, especially during residency/fellowship when salaries are quite low. That said, it is generally easy for most residents to apply for a deferment, which can cover you for up to three years of residency, and also for an unlimited period of time during fellowship training. For others, finances are simply not an issue, either because family is helping with tuition and expenses, or because of other important factors that trump financial concern. Also, loans can often be paid off over extended periods of time without much stress, although at a higher total cost. While it may initially be frightening to consider bearing the weight of $200,000 in student loans, even high totals such as this are reasonable for physicians to pay off, given the average salary rates.

But if you depend on financial aid you should make sure to compare packages from different schools. If you're unhappy with one, don't hesitate to contact the school about your situation. It's not at all uncommon for financial aid offices to adjust packages if a student anticipates hardship, or receives a better offer elsewhere. Also, remember that there are a number of different types of loans, so the total numbers presented in packages can be deceiving. Typically a large component of an offer is composed of UNSUBSIDIZED government loans, which accrue interest while you're still in school, although you typically don't have to start paying them off until you finish with school or your deferment runs out. So while a package may look great at first glance, it may not be your best option in the long run. Talk to a loan officer about it, and get help calculating your total borrowed amount over four years, your projected repayment, etc. It can be very enlightening and helpful.

Location

It is absolutely critical that you're familiar with your own preferences in this regard. It is quite common to hear students talk about applying to a number of schools in a particular area, which becomes quite expensive with application and interview costs, before realizing they would actually be unhappy living there! So make sure you put in lots of time thinking about places you've lived, and find out about places you know little about, even if you're sure you'd like being there. Better safe than sorry! And again, talk to students, because it's easy to get a false impression of life in a particular area after spending only a day or two there for an interview. Also, be sure to go to second look programs if they're offered to get a better idea about life at that school, in that particular area.

To help with this process, here are some specific questions you might want to think about to help flesh out your preferences:

- Where have you lived before?
- What type of climate do you like, and why? Is a change welcomed?
- Are you a city person? Why do you think so/not?
- Do you want to TRY to be? Make sure you test it out somehow!
- What activities do you like? Are they available nearby?
- Do you like a school located on/near its undergraduate campus?
- Other particular things you'd like in a city (music, food, sports, etc.)
- Where would you live? (apartment, townhouse, dorm, etc.)
- What's the cost of living in this area?
- Would you need a car? If so, how expensive is parking?

Personal

Another very common factor in choosing a school involves personal issues regarding things like proximity to family, to a significant other, to a spouse, etc. Concern about how busy one will be in medical school often enters into such decisions as well. What happens if you really love a school in California, but the love of your life lives on the East Coast? Do long distance relationships work in medical school? How busy will you be? Will you have time for this person? These are very common worries that need to be considered during the decision-making process. It's up to you to know what's most important to you and decide accordingly.

Reputation

What's in a name? For some people, a name says lot! Reputation is one of those hotly debated issues, thus some applicants accordingly place a lot of emphasis on it throughout their decision process. And it makes sense. After all most pre-medical students are always working hard, striving to be the best, trying to get papers published, get into honor societies, so it's only natural that they'd also want to attend a school with the most prestige, the most door-opening power, etc. But let's face it, not everyone can go to a Top Five school, and quite honestly, one of those schools might not be the best fit for you. Ultimately, your happiness should be paramount, and if being happy means going to your state school and turning down that Top 10 institution, so be it!

Realistically though, the difficulty of turning down a top school, and the bragging rights that go along with being able to say you went to that famous school everyone knows about, often lead to students making the medical school decision based almost solely on name. And there ARE some reasons why one might want to attend schools with the best reputations. First off, it is commonly said by residents, faculty and residency program directors, that the name on your diploma will help you greatly during the residency match process. For example, many Duke students who recently went through the match process recall having received interview offers literally within minutes of submitting their electronic applications, and knew their applications were not read in their entirety before these offers were extended. Rather, they were extended offers based on their school of attendance. Many reputable sources, such as residency program directors, continually confirm this notion. However, it is also important to remember that those match lists you see everywhere need to be taken with a grain of salt. It seems that every school brags about 90 or so percent of their students getting one of their top three choices. But how do you know what those choices are? Even first-year medical students know little about what residencies are more prestigious, desirable, competitive, etc. How can you be expected to be an expert as an applicant? The answer is, you can't. So don't put too much emphasis on match data, especially since it is hardly an indicator of your happiness for four years. And don't neglect those other critical four factors discussed above.

Decision Tips

Here are some important general points for this process:

- **Show initiative**. Go out of your way to get as much info as you can, both about yourself and the schools you're interested in/accepted at.
- **Start early**. It's never too early to start learning about schools! Talk to advisors at your school, check out web sites, utilize resources like studentdoctor.net, listed in the back of this book.
- **Talk to students at every school**. Pick their brains. More often than not they'll be honest about the ups and downs of their school. When you interview, stay with students if you can. If a school doesn't appear to offer hosting, contact admissions and ask, because most schools do although they often don't advertise it.

- **Go back and visit**. Go to the second look weekend, but remember that it's a "show" of sorts, and might not necessarily be representative of daily life at that school. Don't be quick to judge. Remember that you might be visiting during a really tough week between a string of exams, or maybe you only talked to a certain subset of the class with whom you might not identify. Again, it all comes back to making sure you talk to as many people as possible.

- **If you're playing the waitlist game, don't just settle, stick with it**. Show your top choice school that you want to be a student there more than anything; they'll appreciate it. Write letters, but don't be obnoxious by calling all the time. Be sincere. And remember, your happiness is really important in this process, so be sure to think twice when you're contemplating not taking that last-minute waitlist acceptance just because it means changing your plans, losing a $500 apartment deposit, etc. What's worth more, your happiness or your wallet?

- **Last but not least, don't be afraid to go with your gut feelings.** After all, you know yourself best!

--Tom LeBlanc

How to Judge

Many factors played a role in my choice of a medical school: reputation, location, financial aid, curriculum. But the most important factor was my interaction with the schools themselves, throughout the whole application process. In my opinion, a school's treatment of their applicants is a pretty good indicator of how they tend to treat their students. I always reacted positively when a school treated me well, and found it hard not to think negatively when I was treated like a cow in a herd.

Reputation is worth a lot, but I also wanted to be at a place where I would be happy. When I was applying, I paid close attention to the letters the schools sent out, to web sites, and to how people treated me on the day of my interview. I remember approaching one interview quite unenthusiastically due to a negative first impression I had formed, but then to my surprise being won over by a warm, inquisitive interviewer and friendly medical students.

The most important thing I observed was the attitude of my faculty interviewers. I also noted whether the students seemed happy. Would students help each other, or was it a fiercely competitive environment? In addition, I asked everyone questions about clinical rotations, so I could get a sense of whether students at a particular school had sufficient patient contact, a diverse enough patient population, etc. For it is absolutely critical that you as an applicant know a little about the patient population before joining a medical school, importantly, whether you will see more "bread and butter cases" or more esoteric ones, and to understand which style fits you best. If you would like to be a general practitioner, you should focus on schools that see lots of common cases, but if you know that you would like to pursue a specialty field, look at schools that have clinical training in tertiary medical centers.

Another crucial factor for me was environment. After taking two years off between college and medical school, I was very interested in location, climate and affordability. I wanted to find a place where it would be easy to live, with a short commute and lots of trees. It may sound a little silly, but sometimes seemingly insignificant factors like climate make medical school much more bearable, and ultimately it all comes down to what YOU like. After all, for most people medical school hardly determines the area they will end up settling in, like a residency or future training might. Rather, it is a flexible, open time during which you can really explore a new part of the country. In addition, you might also want to look at whether the school is in close proximity to its undergraduate campus. While this was not one of my main concerns, I thought it might be nice to attend cultural programs on the undergraduate campus, take classes there if I had time, or even eat, work out, and use library facilities there. And after six months in medical school I can guarantee that little factors like these really do affect the environment!

Many people say that curriculum played an important role in their decision, but honestly I wonder how many people really know what things like "problem-based learning," "traditional" and "accelerated pace" mean. However, since our curriculum is drastically different from most schools with only one year of basic science training versus two, an early start to clinical training, and one year dedicated to research or other scholarly pursuits, curriculum was an important factor for many of my classmates. After all, there's a big difference between being in class from 9 a.m.-5 p.m. day in and day out like we have during our first year at Duke, versus a more traditional half-day, two-year lecture schedule at other schools.

When making my decision, curriculum became very important because I knew I wanted to get a Master's in Public Health during medical school. At each of my interviews, I asked about how many students typically pursue second degrees, if their time off was funded or if they had to pay extra tuition, and whether their time off was built into the curriculum. One of the major reasons I came to Duke was that I could get an MPH during my third year without taking more time off!

--Prateeti Khazanie

Making a Choice

Looking back at the way I went about things, the summer before my senior year, I realize that I had no idea what I really wanted in a school or which schools would best suit me. The interview process itself definitely teaches you a lot about these factors, but there are a lot of things you can do beforehand to get a better idea where to even apply in the first place, or what things are important to think about and notice when you visit a school. I applied to 19 schools (started with 15 and kept arbitrarily adding), had 15 interviews (after finally forcing myself to turn down some in the end), received acceptances to 12 schools, and ended up making my decision at the extreme last minute. As I visited schools, I was definitely able to make some kind of crude ranking system in my head. In the end, I think I definitely made the right choice, but thinking back now I realize that Duke was not even on my original AMCAS application! I added it at the last minute without even knowing anything about the program.

So I urge you to start thinking about what might be important to you as early on as you possibly can. Each school has its own benefits in terms of curriculum, finances, reputation and of course, location. And a lot of your preferences and feelings about schools must be sorted out as you visit schools. However, the first major steps should be taken before you even fill out your primary application. In just the past few months I have already seen countless interviewees who are just now learning about Duke's unique curriculum. This is a pretty important detail to know about before you apply, let alone step into an interview!

The easiest first step in educating yourself about schools and their styles is attending the programs that many medical school admissions offices put on at undergraduate institutions. Not all medical schools have these programs, and I believe that is it largely regional, but an admissions officer and several medical students who likely attended your undergrad school will come and speak on the program and many aspects of student life. At the start of my junior year, thinking about medical schools was the last thing on my mind, and as a result, I missed out on many opportunities to learn more about them. So think about it! These events will likely not help you make a final decision on a school, but it is a great time to just get an idea of what types of schools are even out there and what interests you. Are you better suited for a traditional lecture-based curriculum, or would you rather learn via the more innovative problem/case-based format? Would you like to attend a larger school, or does a class size of under a hundred sound about right? Do you want to stay in a city, go to a city, move away from a city or stay away from a city? I applied to, interviewed at and revisited four medical schools in New York City before realizing that I would NEVER survive being a medical student in a city where most of my friends were working and living a completely different life. Admittedly, going through the whole process helped me come to this realization, but it was something that I had not even really considered when I originally applied to these schools.

Another really easy thing to do early on is buy one of those huge books that describe each school in detail (*U.S. News Ultimate Guide to Medical Schools, The Princeton Review's Best 162 Medical Schools*). The ones that are written by medical students can be the most helpful (*Peterson's Insider's Guide to Medical Schools: Current Students Tell You What Their Medical School Is Really Like* is a great one) although the AAMC one is the only "official" one in terms of deadlines, etc. As long as you keep in mind that the write-ups are clearly biased, you can get a lot out of them. Even a really basic book that describes the school in a very dry fashion and gives facts (class size, tuition, location, etc.) can be useful (like the AAMC's book). If a school sounds interesting, call the admissions office and request additional reading material, or even easier, find them on the Web. A lot of schools will not send out information until you get an interview (or even until you are admitted) unless you ask, so don't be shy! Also, contact anyone you know who attends a school that you are interested in. Most people LOVE to talk about their schools, and for the most part, they will be honest about both the positive and the negative aspects of their experience. Educate yourself. And no matter how you do it, do it early on. Do it before you finalize your list of schools.

My last word of advice—do not let any one factor be the deciding factor. Being happy at a school does not just depend on the school's reputation or location or how much you are paying to go there or even the curriculum. You must search for the combination of these factors that best suits your needs, and go with it!

--Sarah Tyler

Case Studies

As the acceptances start to come in, hopefully your first choice school will be on that list. But, maybe you are unsure about which school is your first choice or which one you want to choose amongst your other options. Or, you might be on a couple of waitlists in late July. Perhaps major changes in your personal life have dramatically altered your thinking—just before or even after the deadline for choosing your school.

The circumstances that people find themselves in when choosing schools to apply to, and ultimately to go to, vary widely. These circumstances all represent opportunities. Consider some of the following scenarios:

Passion and performance

- Student A applies to a large number of top-tier schools, directly from a Top 25 liberal arts college. He has a 4.0 GPA, has strong research and athletic experiences and did clinical work like his brother, who is a physician. He is accepted to many schools, and chooses a full scholarship to Duke Medical School over matriculation at Harvard Medical School.
- Student B applies to a large number of top-tier schools, directly from a Top Five liberal arts college. He has good grades, good MCATs and extensive research experience, including his master's work during a fellowship to a university in the United Kingdom. He chooses the Harvard Health Sciences and Technology program over a major scholarship to University of Michigan's medical school.

Take-home messages:

Your grades, MCATs and experiences—including clinical, research or the business work to improve health care—all matter, and will be used to judge you. That is a reality. A top undergraduate university can help get your foot in the door, but isn't a requirement and holds less weight once you are being reviewed by admissions committees. To set yourself up to be able to have flexibility, choices and good financial options, like these people above, work hard. But, do so with a passion to address a particular problem or way of solving problems, not as a way to get into medical schools. Empty grades and MCAT scores, with no sincere undercurrent of public service fools fewer people today. Don't fool yourself, and just engage in the pre-med rat race head down, or you will be unhappy. Try to make the world a better and a healthier place, in a focused way, with an eye towards how pre-medical and ergraduate coursework can help you do so. Then, having choices of where go to medical school will be a by-product of your performance in meeting your own goals, and engaging in the self-guided altruism that makes you happiest.

In fact, if your high performance on pre-medical requirements is done as a by-product of your conviction for your cause(s), the ultimate choice of a medical school may also be easier. You may choose Harvard Medical School because of a specific set of the best researchers in a field could mentor you there; with their training and reputation, you could go on to have the freedom to pursue your own research just as they. Or, you may choose a full scholarship at Duke over going to Harvard, because you have been committed to service in rural Southern towns near family, don't want your residency decision affected by debt and see the clinical experience as equivalent at both places. In making these final choices, note also that friends, family and mentors with experience in medicine (such as my Duke friend's brother), can provide you with substantial guidance IF you ask good questions.

Patience

- A classmate applies to a number of medical schools directly from a top-tier private university. She is accepted to a Top 25 medical school, but holds out to come off the waitlist at Duke Medical School until July, and matriculates there.
- A friend applies to many medical schools directly from a Top Five liberal arts college, with a special emphasis on proximity to family. He has research experience and good MCATs, but not top-tier grades. He is on the waitlist for some time, having applied to a smaller pool of schools, but is eventually accepted off the list and goes to Jefferson Medical School near his family.

Take-home messages:

Don't let the medical school admissions process intimidate you. You are in charge of your decisions. If you are on the waitlist at one of your top choice schools, and a number of factors such as your family living there make it more ideal than other places, be patient and make it clear to that top choice school that you would prefer to go there (call and write a letter).

On another note, *U.S. News and World Report* rankings are realistic factors to consider in that higher ranked schools tend to have more resources and more options for doing research and varied clinical electives; but don't just rely on them. Do research and talk to current physicians and residents to develop a sense of what you want out of you life and career. Medical school will help you better define that, but knowing in advance will help you with applications, choosing a school and getting into residency by focusing your efforts in medical school towards your future path. Do you want to be an academic who changes the way the system works with your basic or clinical research? Are you going to try to go into a competitive residency like ophthalmology, dermatology or neurosurgery? Or do you want to focus on your patients, your clinical practice of the future in perhaps primary care or emergency medicine, and spend more time with your family? If the latter, the rank of the school matters less, as there are a reasonably high number of slots for certain residencies.

When applying to medical schools, and selecting from your acceptances, assess what the drivers of your contentment are. If you don't know, that's okay, but invest some time in stepping away from some of the pre-med requirements for a moment, and in researching your longer-term trajectory. You can't go wrong with any top-tier school because they have a broad set of resources and potential mentors, but if you understand more about yourself, then you'll see how the particular school itself, and its reputation, becomes a much smaller fraction of the reason why you go there.

Perseverance

- An acquaintance applies to only a few top medical schools directly from her large undergraduate university. She is not accepted to any schools. She does research for a year, applies again and is accepted to Columbia Medical School.
- A friend applies to a large number of medical schools directly from a Top Five liberal arts college. His grades and initial MCAT score are not ideal for top-tier schools, so is not accepted to any schools. He takes time off, gains additional clinical experience and retakes the MCATs. He is accepted to Cornell's Medical School in his second application attempt.

Take-home messages:

First, apply to a sufficient number of schools the first year around, and understand the places you're applying to. Apply to a fairly large number of schools you would be happy at, or are going to learn more about on the general AMCAS application. If the expense is high for you and your family's income, definitely apply for a fee waiver. Then, as secondary applications come in, make sure you've already started to complete your research on the schools, and start to be more disciplined about which applications you complete. Use the essays on the secondary applications as an opportunity to discover more about your interests, your future path, and whether or not the school seems to support those things. Be prepared to interview for at least five to 10 schools, particularly if you are applying to MD/PhD programs, and schedule interviews in geographical clusters, giving yourself more time to visit those places, if you can. It's not often you have an excuse to travel to lots of often new and interesting environments that can open your eyes to new slants on how people live. The research you put into your secondary applications will not only aid you, but make your applications and interviews stronger (and that's one of the reasons schools put you through them).

Second, don't be shy about taking time off to gain new experiences after college and to improve your credentials such as MCATs and clinical experiences, as well as your understanding of your path. Some do this before applying in the first place, and others find themselves in the position of not getting in the first time around. Whether you choose it, or your hand is forced, relish the time between being an undergraduate and starting medical school. It is often the first time in people's lives when they are not under the wing of their parents, nor the wing of an educational institution. Yet, taking just "a couple years off" from school is different than jumping into a career. You can do good work in your temporary job without needing to put in unnecessary face time to impress the boss. Or maybe you don't need to do a traditional job at all, and might be doing some travel-related research. In either case, there are few times in life when both the protection, and the time pressures of parents and/or schools are lifted (it returns with medical school), and people often see themselves for who they really are, and can become, for the first time in these situations. When they finally do apply to medical school, people who have taken productive time away from school are often among the most interesting, thoughtful and self-guided medical students.

So, if you're not ready to apply, not ready to choose (you can defer, but respect that others are also vying for slots) or don't get into medical school the first time, persevere, be patient and perform new activities with passion, after your undergraduate work.

--Jason Langheier

OTHER CONSIDERATIONS

The Nontraditional Applicant

CHAPTER 10

Are you a little different from the average applicant? Fear not, no medical school admissions committee can discriminate against you—it's against the law. For example, the typical "right-out-of-college" applicant has no real advantage over those applying after taking time off. In fact, almost half of our medical school class took some time off between undergrad and medical school. Is it an advantage? Well, that all depends on what you did during this time, and your reason for applying. Do you want a career change at this point? What's wrong with your job now? Will your family endure the grueling years of medical training? Mindful consideration of these issues can make or break your application.

According to the AAMC, the mean age of matriculants to allopathic medical schools in 2005 was 24 years for men and 23 years for women. This means that most students applying to school are one or two years out of college. However, by some estimates, as many as one-fifth of applicants to medical school are older than 27 years old. Students applying at 27, or even 47, years of age have experiences from all walks of life. This broad spectrum of ages makes defining the "non-traditional" applicant (NTA) a little problematic. NTAs were conventionally characterized as anyone who wasn't matriculating to medical school in the semester following their graduation from college. NTAs were characterized as anyone who graduated early, took time off or ventured into a career before applying to medical school. For the purposes of this book, however, we will define the term slightly differently. In this chapter, we will discuss the experiences of older applicants, those that graduated in three years of college and applied early, international students and even those who have started a family before beginning medical school.

--Aaron Lesher

Starting Early

Unlike the majority of students in my class, I took the fast track when it came to applying to medical school. Accumulating enough advanced placement credits in high school, I was able to graduate from Rensselaer Polytechnic Institute with a degree in biology in only three years. I chose not to take time off, but rather took my MCAT during the spring of my second year and began to apply to medical schools the summer after my second year. The whole process went by very quickly, and before I knew it, I was a first-year student at Duke University School of Medicine. Since then, I have had plenty of time to evaluate my application process, as well as the advantages and disadvantages of starting medical school so quickly.

I was first convinced that medicine would be an ideal profession for me in high school, and this is what prompted me to choose biology as my major in college. Because the requirements for my biology degree were identical to the requirements for medical school, I had no difficulty fulfilling all of these requirements in three years, with plenty of time remaining to take several economics, psychology and literature classes. Taking the MCAT in the spring semester of my second year was ideal. During that semester, I was in the midst of taking Organic Chemistry II, Physiology and Molecular Biology. These classes warmed me up for the exam, and I found that studying for the MCAT was not as difficult as I had previously imagined.

When I was applying to medical school, I was worried that the schools would think that I was not prepared or mature enough to handle the workload and emotional stresses involved in medicine. In my fast track, I did not have time to study in a foreign country or major in something other than biology. Then I realized that applicants who finish college so quickly are rare and that in itself would make me stand out. In addition, maturity is not always defined by the number of experiences, but rather by what a person takes from those experiences.

The actual process of applying and interviewing was not unique for me. I filled out my AMCAS application and secondary applications just like any other traditional medical school applicant. There were no questions that were repeatedly asked of me during my interviews. Nevertheless, I walked into each interview prepared to explain why I felt I was mature enough to begin medical school and prepared to explain all of the experiences I took advantage of during my three years of college.

There are many benefits of finishing college in three years and beginning medical school right away. Not only did I save a full year of college tuition, but I also feel that I am one step ahead in my career. I will be able to begin the next phase of my life a little earlier than most other people. The road to becoming a physician is a long one, and I was fortunate enough to grab myself some extra time at the end of it. Furthermore, in many ways I feel medical school is merely an extension of college. Every day that I go to class, I still feel like I am a college student.

Every so often, I also think about the disadvantages of my decision to start medical school so quickly. I know that I am going to have the rest of my life to work, so why am I in such a rush to start? The best time to explore my life, my talents, my dreams and my ambitions would have been now, at a younger age. I sometimes wonder if it would have been best to have taken time off after college to do the things that I know I will never be able to do in the future. In addition, my college years were so important to me, because it was there that I really "grew up." I learned a lot about myself and made some amazing friends.

All in all, maturity is the answer to whether finishing college early and starting medical school immediately is the right decision for you. If you feel confident that medicine is a perfect match for you and that you are ready to take on all of the responsibilities of becoming a medical student/physician, do not hesitate to begin your future immediately. Based on my values and personality, I am very satisfied with my decision—I am fascinated by the things I have learned, the people I have met and the friends I have made.

Finishing college in three years also means that you should take advantage of every opportunity that flashes in front of you. Use summer vacations to work or volunteer in areas that will strengthen your commitment to society and/or medicine. Begin research projects that interest you early in college and stick with them. Join activities that you find enjoyable and strive to do them well. Stay involved in your community and try new things. In the end, you will prepare yourself for the rigors of medical school, and become more aware of the issues you, as a physician, might need to address in the future.

--Priya Batra

Dealing with a Late Start

I noted that my interviewer was scribbling intently as I sat across from him in his moderate sized, neutral toned office. This was my first interview and I was exceptionally nervous. His scribbling while we were talking only added to my angst. What was he doing? Finally he stopped, looked up at me and then, with a smile, he presented what had so obviously distracted him from our supposed conversation. To my dismay, he had drawn a graph of his perception of my current financial status, and what he was sure would be my long-term finances should I pursue this crazy course of attending medical school over the age of 30. With academic debt clouding midlife, retirement age pushed to 80 and essentially never fully recovering, he wanted to know if I was insane!

It was this experience that led me to do a little research on age and acceptance to medical school. I was saddened when I found that people past a certain age are significantly less likely to gain acceptance than their younger counterparts. One Web source documented a 42 percent acceptance rate for people under 32, while those over 32 had a 26 percent acceptance rate, albeit acknowledging that there may be potential confounders. I knew that I would have to justify my reason for a career change, but I actually thought my age might be an advantage in the application process. After all, I had a graduate degree, publications, an obviously strong work ethic and the knowledge and skills from another profession that happens to be in health care, demonstrating my knowledge of what I was getting into. Perhaps most importantly, I had some of that wisdom that only comes with age. These factors seemed not to matter to most schools; the negative aspects of being over 30 came up in almost every interview, Duke being one of the exceptions. I would recommend to anyone in their 30s to be prepared to defend the value of being an older applicant and develop strategies to redirect the conversation so that it does not consume the interview.

The application process posed other challenges. Studying for the MCAT while being employed full-time was a hardship. There were folks in my MCAT prep course who had taken a semester off for the sole purpose of MCAT preparation, and even those currently enrolled in school still had more time than I to donate to studying. Moreover, these people had recently taken physics, chemistry, etc., whereas it had been more than 10 years for me. Needless to say, I was a bit intimidated by the fact that they would determine my ranking on MCAT scoring. I did have a good experience with taking the Kaplan prep course, though. The structure that the course offered and the review of basic sciences were particularly useful since I was many years post-undergraduate education.

Now that I am fully entrenched in this academic process, I have found that I cannot study as relentlessly as I did in my previous endeavors. My responsibilities are greater, and my perspective on what is truly important in life has changed. I have a husband who is also in medical school, a mortgage, a dog, two cats and far too many fish. Moreover, I work part-time to help minimize my debt. Regardless of age, recognizing that I had some additional responsibilities and planning how to manage those prior to matriculating has been key to maintaining my sanity.

Despite some of the difficulties in applying and attending medical school over 30, I would recommend it to anyone who finds themselves developing an interest in medicine after passing the traditional age. No doubt the age factor and the associated changes in lifestyle are a hurdle. However, you will grow older no matter what you do; why not pursue your aspirations in the process?

--Noelle DeSimone

The 180

I was 24 years old and programming for NASA in a tiny, out-of-the-way basement cubicle when I realized something was missing from my career; if I wanted to, I could spend the entire day without interacting with another human being! Then one night I rushed a friend to the emergency room and the following month I took care of the same friend after surgery. While I was in the hospital and talking with the nurses, residents and doctors, I realized that health care workers enjoy an element of humanism in their career. The more I thought about it, medicine seemed like a career with all the enticements of my previous work (research and technical challenges) but also had the element of care-giving that was missing from my previous career as a computer programmer. I decided to figure out what I needed to apply to medical school.

It was a long haul. Once I decided that I wanted to study medicine in early 1999, it took about two and a half years for me to actually start medical school! There were two things that I had to do before applying. First, I had to fulfill all the academic pre-med requirements, which took the entire fall 1999, spring 2000 and summer 2000 semesters. Once I finished the required class work, I took the Kaplan MCAT course and took the MCAT in August 2000. I could have applied to schools to matriculate in 2001, but I did not know if I would do well enough on the MCAT. So I waited until I got the results before I saw my pre-med advisor from my undergraduate university, Duke (this happened around April 2001). During the summer of 2001, I submitted the AMCAS primary around mid-July (a little too late) and then submitted the secondary applications in late September and early November (way too late). Because I worked a full-time job throughout the whole application process (except for a two-week break to prepare for the MCAT) it was a really hard time for me. Most other aspects of my life suffered as a result. My social life was most severely affected.

To post-bacc or not to post-bacc?

Once I decided that I wanted to study medicine, I had to take four classes to fulfill the pre-med requirements. Because my undergraduate degree was in engineering, I had already taken the physics, math and basic chemistry requirements. However, I still had to take four classes: two semesters of organic chemistry and two semesters of biology. The most important thing I did, however, was to make sure that I thought I would actually like medicine. From where I stood, there seemed to be two ways of fulfilling the requirements: going to a post-baccalaureate pre-med program or taking the classes at night. My job was not that flexible, so I couldn't take classes during the day. Because I only had four classes to fulfill, I thought it would be pretty easy to take the classes at night. I thought that the overhead of a post-bacc program was too great: I would have to apply to a post-bacc program, quit my job to attend school full-time just to apply to medical school, then find work again throughout the application process.

How could I know that a career change was right for me?

Immediately after I thought about a career change, I started to doubt my decision. I wasn't sure if I would enjoy medicine at all. To find out if I would like clinical medicine, I shadowed various health care professionals in different departments through a summer program in a local hospital before work and on the weekends. The shadowing went well despite the fact that I almost fainted the first time I saw a nurse draw blood! Since I enjoyed the hospital and wanted to get some real-life experience, I took a course and got certified to be an EMT. I loved the course so much, especially the ambulance ride-along experience, that I started working part-time on the same ambulance that I did the ride-along with. The EMT cxperience was very valuable and helped me a lot in understanding the cardiac physiology we learned in our first year.

I didn't get the best grades as a freshman in undergraduate.

Because I took my basic chemistry as a freshman, I had accumulated some "red-flag" marks in those pre-med classes. However, I felt that admissions committees would overlook my bad marks because I was an older applicant. My post-bacc pre-med grades were fine, as was my MCAT score, so I was able to make up for my freshman grades.

Which schools to apply to?

When I was choosing which medical schools to apply to, I made a pretty big mistake. At first, I planned to apply to a bunch of MD/PhD programs and had picked out a list of about 12 appropriate schools to apply to. When it came time for the online AMCAS application, I got really scared because I realized that I would be about 35 years old upon finishing an MD/PhD program. So I ended up designating only the MD program choice on the AMCAS application, but I kept the same list that I was considering for the MD/PhD degree. The problem with this approach was that I ended up applying to about seven state schools for their MD program, which were all very hard to get into from out of state. I only got an interview at one out of the seven state schools, and of the private schools that I applied to, only one school did not offer me an interview. I therefore recommend applying to state schools (of your own state) and to private schools for the MD program, advice that I already knew but ended up ignoring with my last-minute switch in application procedure.

My last piece of advice is to try to stay with a student host during interviews and second look weekends. I made the mistake of thinking, "I am too old to sleep on someone's floor." But getting the student perspective can be very beneficial in helping pick a school. Of course, if you have a bad experience with a student, you shouldn't let that totally influence your decision.

A complete career change is not unheard of among those considering medical school. Going from any job into the field of medicine can be a big change. Just be sure to look closely at what lies ahead before deciding medicine is for you.

--Joshua Unger

Getting Away

Perhaps the biggest mistake college pre-med s make is getting caught up in the "career game:" do well in college so you can get into medical school so you can pass the boards so you can get into a residency program so you can. At some point it becomes obvious that the path to an MD requires us to jump through a seemingly endless series of academic hoops. During my senior year of college, I asked myself if I was ready to keep jumping and, to my surprise, I admitted that I wasn't. My story, then, is for you pre-med s who want to temporarily disengage from your career ambitions in the hopes of one day returning to them with a clearer sense of purpose and determination.

After graduating from college I decided that I needed travel money, so I got a job as a research and development engineer in the medical device industry, made some lucky stock trades at the height of the dot-com economy, and lived frugally for a year and a half. Finances secured, I quit my job, packed my bags, said my goodbyes and left town. Having been a fan of Kerouac in college, I started my adventures by traveling the highways of America in my '83 Volvo, hiking and camping at every national park I could find. Along the way, I turned to artwork and converted a friend's garage into a studio from which I produced quite a few paintings, some of which I even ended up selling. After 13,745 miles I had my first full beard and a strong desire to see the world beyond America's borders. I had successfully evolved from stressed pre-med student into wandering bohemian.

After America, I traveled the rails of Europe for a while, staying with relatives and friends, then moved on to Asia. While trekking in the Himalayas, I had the opportunity to visit a small medical clinic run by volunteer physicians from the Himalayan Rescue Association. Situated at the foot of the snow-capped Annapurnas and a week's walking distance from the nearest telephone or car-accessible road, the clinic received all of its donated supplies via donkeys and porters. Even in such austere conditions, the Alaskan doctor running the clinic clearly loved providing basic healthcare to the local Nepalese. This was medicine in its purest, most fundamental form: a person trying to heal with only her wits, a few essential instruments and some basic drugs. I was truly inspired, and decided that I needed to do something similar.

So shortly thereafter I found myself volunteering to help operate a small, isolated medical clinic for six months in South America that served the Wapishana Amerindians, a tribe of subsistence farmers and hunters who live off the savannah in essentially the same manner as did their ancestors. The facility itself, 120 miles from any telephone or paved road in a malaria-infested region of Guyana, was a rough group of tin-roofed buildings that had no running water, one radio transmitter for contact with the outside world and a population of fruit bats living in the halls. I had the time of my life to say the least. Upon my return to the United States, the impending academic hoops didn't loom so large once I realized how desperately I wanted to be a doctor.

Apparently my five-year disappearance from the career/academic radar screen placed me in the "non-traditional applicant" category when I finally got around to applying to medical school. Don't let the title bother you, because once you're in medical school hunched over a textbook trying to memorize which cranial nerve innervates the trapezius muscle you'll be thanking yourself for having taken time off. What I chose to do with my five years between college and medical school is definitely not for everyone. But for those of you who are wary of the time and discipline needed for becoming a doctor, and who also happen to enjoy a little adventure, I highly recommend a vacation for as long as needed. Take your time, there's no rush, it's your life and you write the story. And remember that even with the most careful planning, life will always be a series of improvisations, as it should be.

--Kitch Wilson

Family First

For years I felt I had a good idea of where I wanted my life to go and what my goals were. I had known for years that I wanted to complete college and attend medical school. I also knew that, at some point in the mix, I wanted to start a family. However, I was not sure at what point that was going to happen. Suddenly, standing there in the labor and delivery suite of the hospital, seeing my wife hold our newborn daughter, I knew that everything had changed. That family had now been formed, we were no longer just a couple and every decision we made from that point on would also affect this precious, new creature in our lives. Looking back, I can honestly say it was a change for the best.

Applying to and attending medical school with the added responsibilities of a family can certainly seem like a daunting task. While it does offer some distinct and unique challenges, it also can prove to be an extremely rewarding experience.

I have been married for nearly five years now, and my wife and I are the proud parents of two little girls who truly are the joys of our lives and keep us on our toes. As I was preparing for and applying to medical school, I constantly had to consider how my future plans would affect my family. My wife understood my desire to attend medical school and supported me fully. This was (and still is) one of the most important decisions I have ever made. Medical school is really an incredible challenge, and the application process is a challenge in and of itself.

One of the most important considerations we had to take into account was where we would apply. There are a lot of fantastic medical schools that are either in some rather unsavory locations, or in some areas with an outrageous cost of living. With a family, these were both important considerations. It is expensive to apply to medical school, and I had no desire to spend money applying to schools that were in areas that just wouldn't be conducive to raising a family.

Having a family and, at least in my case, working full-time while completing one's undergraduate work can prevent one from participating in as many extracurricular activities as others who are applying. This can at first seem to be a detriment, but I actually found it to be a strength. Marriage and children require an enormous amount of maturity and dedication, both qualities that medical schools are really seeking in applicants. In my interviews, I was treated very favorably and was told on multiple occasions that the interviewer was impressed with my maturity. I really feel that this is something that one gains through life experiences, and simply cannot be taught. Even though I may not have done the fantastic internships that others had, or had not been involved in as many different organizations, my own life experiences proved to be just as invaluable.

I also thought it was important that my wife visit some of the schools at which I interviewed. When it came time to make the decision, it was much easier for my wife as she was familiar with the schools and areas we were deciding between and was able to contribute more to the decision.

Medical school with a family has also been an interesting challenge thus far, but there have also been some great advantages. Time with my family has helped me to learn better how to prioritize and also how to use my time more effectively. I have honestly had sufficient time to study, as well as still be involved with my family. I also feel I am fortunate to have a family to go home to and share things with, as they are an anchor for me.

Medical school is full of challenges as well as rewards. Having a family through the entire process has only made this stage of my life that much more rewarding. Many medical schools celebrate diversity in their student body and having students at different stages of life with different backgrounds helps add to this diversity. While the challenges are present, they are certainly surmountable and can even be enjoyable as I share them with my family.

--Peter Jones

The International Experience

Both Wendy (my twin sister) and I finished our college education in China and came to the United States for graduate studies. My college major was biology and Wendy's was chemistry. We both enrolled in a PhD program in biology in the United States and lived on full scholarships. During the second year of her graduate school, Wendy decided to quit and go to medical school. I continued my graduate studies until I got my PhD in Genetics. Both Wendy and I finally got into medical schools in the U.S. Since Wendy was a couple of years ahead of me in the process, I got most of my advice from her.

I was surprised to learn that all the undergraduate courses we took in China would not be recognized by medical schools in the U.S. So when I was still a graduate student at Cold Spring Harbor Lab in Long Island, I went to UC-

Berkley and took most of my pre-med courses there while I was writing my PhD dissertation.

In terms of extracurricular/volunteer activities, we had the advantage of being bilingual. Most hospitals needed volunteer medical interpreters. Volunteering as a medical interpreter was not only a rewarding experience for me but also gave me the opportunity to observe directly the practice of medicine.

Going to medical school was not realistic for me until the last year of my graduate school when I was, like many other students and scholars from mainland China, granted a green card due to the Tiananmen Square massacre. Like most international students, I came here on a F1 (student) visa and was not eligible for any government-sponsored financial aid for medical students. Although I did meet a student from mainland China who managed to borrow $100,000 from her relatives and friends to go to medical school, I do not have any relatives or friends who would be able to help me financially for medical education. So for most international students who come from a poor developing country and want to go to medical school in the U.S., the first step will have to be getting a green card. Once you have this, you are generally treated by medical schools as if you were a U.S. citizen. For the rest of this discussion, international students refers to those who are on any kind of visa (typically an F1 visa). It does not apply to those that hold a green card.

Most of the prerequisites for entering medical school are the same for both U.S. citizens and international students. International students are required to have a bachelor's degree, take the MCAT and apply through AMCAS. Statistics show that the majority of the international students who gain admission to accredited medical schools in the U.S. have completed their undergraduate degree in this country. However, in some circumstances, degrees from other countries have been recognized though even in these instances, most medical schools prefer that you do at least a year of additional tertiary education in the U.S. before applying.

Despite the similarities in the application process, there are differences. For example, at many medical schools, the TOEFL is required for students whose native language is not English. Sometimes this requirement can be substituted by humanities classes taken in college or the MCAT. Such policies are different for each medical school. One of the most significant differences that international students face is in the financial aid policy. International students do not qualify for federal aid including things like Stafford loans nor do they often qualify for need-based aid from the medical institution either. Exceptions to this general rule include the MSTP program (MD/PhD) as well as merit scholarships offered by some medical schools.

There has also been a recent trend amongst many of the elite medical schools to offer unsubsidized need-based loans (but not grants) to attract more international students. That being said, most international medical students in the U.S. are funded by international scholarships or personal finances or both.

Once you have taken the MCAT, completed (or are completing) college, and have made plans on how to fund medical school, you are now ready to apply! Though gaining admission to medical school in the U.S. is difficult for any student, unfortunately, it is even more difficult for international students. However, it is nowhere near as impossible as many contend, so take everything with a grain of salt. At present, I know several international students in medical school and statistics say that more than 100 international students gain admission to medical school every year. That being said, out of the 126 or so accredited medical schools in United States, international students can apply to fewer than 50 of them (even that's being generous). Most of the state medical schools in the U.S. will not even accept applications from international students (though some will accept your application fee, so check up on this before you apply!). The policies of state schools were not surprising because I was told this by my pre-medical advisor and it is common knowledge. However, what was surprising is that many private medical schools also do not accept international students. Examples include New York University, George Washington University and Saint Louis University just to name a few, but the list is longer than that. Call the admissions office or buy the annual *U.S. News* medical school rankings and statistics guide and look up which schools accepted any international students.

Once you have determined which schools you want/can apply to, you have completed an important part of the process. The procedure of filling out the AMCAS and the secondaries are similar for both U.S. and foreign students. The next step where issues unique to international students come up is at the interview stage. In addition to the typical topics that come up at interviews, a few topics might come up that are unique to international students. For example, if your country of origin has a socialized system of health care, it is reasonable for your interviewer to ask you advantages and disadvantages of that system. Other common questions include why you want to study in the U.S., if you plan to go back to your home country after medical school and whether you will be able to adjust socially and culturally in medical school especially if you did not do your undergraduate degree here. But there are some positives. Many international students coming from different cultures and from countries of different economic backgrounds often bring new perspectives that are valued by admissions officers trying to build an all-round medical class. Do not be afraid to highlight the differences that you bring as an international student.

--Qinghong Yang and Srinivas Peddi

Minority Report

I remember staring at the composite photo and thinking "only two black people?!" Out of class of 150 medical school students, how was it they had only managed to "build" a minority community of such small capacity? The hairstyles and clothing of the faces I was staring into were not outlandishly out of date, so there was no way that I could fool myself in thinking that the picture was decades old. The year 2001 in bold letters clearly confirmed that this was the current class, but I still couldn't believe it. I had just spent a good 30 minutes talking with the Director of Multicultural Affairs and being convinced that this school would help me develop as a future physician. But how was I to develop in such a homogenous community? How would anyone thrive, even those in the majority? I had always believed that the more we are exposed to people different from us, the more open we become to the differences that make each one of us individuals. It was clear to me as I reviewed my visit to the school that I would "be" the diversity at that school, instead of "contributing" to the diversity of the school, and I didn't think that I would be comfortable choosing a school knowing such information.

In looking back at the entire medical school application experience, one of things I regret most is that I didn't pay attention to ALL the details. During those summer months when you're picking schools to apply to, it can be very easy to be attracted to the more visible numbers like tuition rates, size of class, board scores and rank order. I think my experience serves as a good example that there are other numbers that you should think about that might not be so readily available to you, like the number of international students or the racial make-up of the class. Sometimes these numbers will be nearly impossible to find. When I came back from that disappointing interview trip, I made a point to looking onto that school's web site. While the school did have a section that was specifically addressed to minority applicants, they never broke down the percentage numbers or described what services they offered to their students of color. Omissions like that should be something you pay attention to in picking schools EARLY in the application process, not after you apply. It will save you both time and money if diversity is an important issue to your personal development.

Minority status in general can be an everyday struggle. Minority status in medical school can only add to the pressures. Finding a supportive student and faculty community can be a great help during the turbulence of medical school, and it seems only worth it to make that extra effort to seek the information you need to make a more informed decision. This extra effort may involve some phones calls to the schools, seeking the advice of current students in the school or doing some extra reading. For example, the American Association of Medical Colleges publishes a book every year that compiles the results of a survey given to every U.S. medical school about their minority opportunities. It's advertised as listing information about minority admissions (number applied, accepted, matriculated and graduated), recruiting efforts, financial opportunities and academic support. It is a publication that I probably would have found very helpful in the past. Additionally, a link off their web site (http://www.aamc.org/students) called "Minorities in Medicine" provides access to great resources like scholarship information, recommended publications, career fairs and links to various minority professional organizations.

I ultimately ending up choosing to accept the Duke offer because along with financial aid, board scores and rank order, a commitment to diversity also proved to be one of their more visible numbers. I knew in choosing to come here that I would be adding to the diversity in a way that would only aid my development. I've been pleased to find that the case during my time here. Aside from race, our class is made up of a wide diversity of religions, positions in life, ideas and experiences. In our Multicultural Resource Center, I have found an extremely supportive staff continually working to bring in speakers to expose the school to a number of topics from religion to sexual orientation. Moreover, I have seen the admissions office's active efforts to maintain and exceed the level of diversity at Duke today, assuring us all that "only two black students" will never be an adequate number.

--Emma Archibong

A Criminal Record

As I slopped hog manure around my school grounds, the last thing on my mind was explaining the incident to medical school deans. Having just graduated high school, my friends and I were merely intent on carrying out an unforgettable senior prank. We had carefully planned our attack. Liquid hog manure would be disgusting and stinky, but not actually detrimental to school property. It was, after all, just fertilizer. The school administrators and local police disagreed, however. After a short investigation (during which they actually traced the manure back to my farm) my cohorts and I were charged with felony criminal mischief.

Having already been accepted to college, I found the charge annoying but not terribly worrisome. I negotiated with the courts and was given a monetary fine and ordered to perform 80 hours of community service. I had all but forgotten the incident when I first sat down to fill out my medical school applications.

The exact wording of the criminal history question varies by school; some requiring you to divulge only crimes you'd been convicted of, while others wanting everything you've ever been charged with. Additionally, just to scare applicants a bit more, the fine print always warns that a complete, in-depth criminal background check will be performed and any discrepancies found will be grounds for revocation of admission.

While I was by no means a jailbird, I was definitely worried about the effect of my record on my chances for admission. Because of the background check (and ethical obligations), however, lying was obviously not an option. After checking the 'yes' box, I set about the difficult process of explaining my answer. I did my best to recount my transgressions in the least damaging way. I also weaved in what I had learned from my mistakes, and how I had repaid my debt to the community. Although I felt as if I was committing application suicide, I sent off my applications.

Luckily, this was not the end; I was delighted to receive numerous interviews. As expected, in most (but not all) of my interviews, I was asked to explain the incident further. Retelling the story good-naturedly and with a bit of humor always worked to my advantage. I found that it was an excellent way of breaking the ice and also gave the interview a friendly, conspiratorial tone. Not a single interviewer seemed to take offense or react negatively. In fact, more than one interviewer shared his own story of youthful criminal exploits.

While those of you with clean records can thank your lucky stars, check 'no,' and move on, the rest of you needn't cringe as you check 'yes.' Remember, you don't really have a choice anyhow. Also, if presented in the correct light, your history can be a bonus. Just be honest, while still attempting to frame your mistake in the best possible light. Offer an explanation, but not an excuse. If you were simply young and stupid, say so. If you planned and strategized while weighing the benefits and risks—knowingly accepting the consequences of your actions—then say so. Also share what you learned, without being cliché, and how you repaid your debt to society (community service is never a bad thing). Mistakes are human, and if framed correctly, your transgressions can make you an interesting and more memorable applicant. Need more proof? One of my interviewers actually referenced slopping manure in my acceptance letter!

--Brooke Rosonke

The Gap Year

CHAPTER 11

At the end of every pre-med 's undergraduate career comes that question—should I take a year off? It's a tough decision. This chapter is designed to give you some insight into the various factors to consider when making your decision. You can learn much for one year out of school, but it can also be beneficial to take that plunge into med school right after undergrad. In this chapter, you will also see what factors to consider should you be faced with the prospect of having to reapply.

If you are considering deferring, each medical school handles requests for deferring matriculation in its own way. Some schools do not even require the applicant to give a reason for why they want to take the year off. Others, like the University of California-San Francisco, require that the applicant be pursuing an opportunity that would pass by should they decide not to enter school that year. Finally, some schools only require a good reason following a certain date, which is usually June 1. This is also the date by which you should have requested deferral at most medical schools.

Discuss the matter with your school after you have been accepted. Simply call the admissions department and ask about their policy regarding deferring for a year. One detail that usually holds true across schools is that they only like to give you one year. If you're thinking about taking two years, it may be best to wait and apply later. Most schools will require you to write a letter detailing why you want to defer, even if it is not any grandiose plan. Your letter will then be reviewed by an admissions officer at the school, and they will send you a letter either rejecting or accepting your request.

If the school does allow you to defer, they will give you information regarding forms you have to fill out and when to send them in. In the case of Duke, I had to fill out part of the AMCAS application for the next year so that they had my name on file. I did not have to pay to file the application, though. The process, if successful, is pretty painless.

A separate process that you may be considering is transferring from one medical school to another. What if you are accepted to a school that was not very high on your list but rejected at one that you really wanted to attend? Would it be possible to do very well in the first year and apply for a transfer? The answer to the last question is highly program dependent. Currently Duke has a blanket statement rejecting all transfers. The major reasons for this are 1) the curriculum is very different from that any other program; and 2) space in classrooms, labs and on ward services (internal medicine, surgery, etc.) is limited. Most schools struggle with space limitations and like to keep their classes at a certain size to ensure a quality learning experience. This is only going to become more of an issue as the Association of American Medical Colleges is asking schools to add spots to their classes. After you have received all your responses from various schools and think that you might want to attempt a transfer, first look up both school's transfer policies. Do not set your hopes too high, and remember, you can receive a great education at any accredited U.S. medical school.

--Jesse Waggoner

A Break from the Ordinary

Burnout. I guess that is the main reason that I decided to take a year off. I was sick of school. I needed a break. The way I looked at it, I had been in school for my entire life, as far back as I could remember, and I'd never had any significant amount of time as a mature adult to simply relax, forget about academics and do something "off the wall." Thus, I decided to defer my acceptance to medical school.

Applying to medical school ahead of time and then deferring for a year was advantageous in two ways. First, I wouldn't have to worry about spending time during my year off to complete lengthy secondary applications for 10 or more schools. Second, and most importantly, the travel-intense interviewing process wouldn't dictate where I would have to live. That is to say, if I wanted to go hang out somewhere else in the world for part of the year, which I did, it would certainly be difficult and enormously expensive to get back to the States for interviews. Once I had deferred, I proceeded with plans for my year-long vacation.

I knew from the start that I wanted absolutely nothing to do with science or medicine during my free year. Many people who take time off before starting medical school choose to work in a hospital or do research of some kind, but I wasn't interested in gaining experience or getting published. I was interested in doing something fun and different.

To achieve that end I decided to pursue my passion for traveling. I applied for and received a post-graduate scholarship to study at the University of Burgos in Burgos, Spain. As an undergrad I had already studied for a semester in Salamanca, Spain, and I desperately wanted to return to that country. I knew that a free year after college would most likely be my last opportunity to spend a significant chunk of time living abroad. Moreover, I love Spanish and I love speaking a second language, so living in Spain afforded me the perfect opportunity to improve my Spanish speaking skills. I took humanities courses in history and language, in no way associated with science or medicine.

The largest chunk of my year off was spent in Spain, but I also worked as a carpenter for several months in Montana, framing houses, hotels and ski lodges. During my childhood I loved constructing things, and throughout high school and college I gained considerable experience in the construction industry by working for home builders during the summer. In Montana, I improved my vocational skill and made a good bit of money. I also hiked and did some light traveling around the area.

My year off between undergrad and medical school was one of the best experiences of my life. It refreshed and motivated me for the start of my medical education. Many pre-med s will opt to jump right into their medical training, and that's fine, but a year off can be highly beneficial for some. My free year helped shape me into the person I am today and taught me a lot about the way I want to practice medicine in the future. I plan to be an internationally-oriented physician, using my language skills and medical knowledge to work in underdeveloped countries in Latin America as well as to improve access to care for underserved parts of the Spanish-speaking community within the United States. My advice to all pre-med s is this: if you're thinking about taking a year off, go for it, but be creative. You should do something fun and adventurous, something that you probably won't ever have another opportunity to do. It is one year...make the most of it.

--W. Chad Hembree

Deferring and Bouncing

Some of the best things in life seem like accidents. When I decided as a junior that I would write my Medical Scientist Training Program (MSTP, discussed further in Chapter 12) applications during the fall of my senior year, I had no intention of applying for post-baccalaureate scholarships. Lab work and medical school were far more important.

Late in the summer, I received a postcard in my mailbox from one of the deans: Brandeis had been invited to submit applications for the Winston Churchill Scholarship, a one-year scholarship for scientists to study at Cambridge University. I was intrigued and spent some time talking to the dean about it and then searching the Cambridge web pages for interesting research. When I found the descriptions of the brain imaging that involved the neurosurgery department, I was hooked. I started to work on the scholarship application and to wonder what would happen if I received the award. Would a medical school let me defer? Would I have to reapply?

By late April I knew that I was going to Duke and that I was going to England, so I wrote Duke and told them that I would defer for a year. Since the English school year starts later than our year, my summer was almost two months longer than normal and I flew to England in late September.

People rave about going abroad and encountering other cultures, so I won't. It took me about five seconds to get used to "the wrong side of the road" and seven or eight months to adequately appreciate the subtle, rich beauty of the land in Cambridgeshire. It was also wonderful to see a different laboratory organization and to interact with an immediate medical environment while working in basic science. My reading was fairly intense since I had no background in neuro-anything, but I was free to add a theoretical investigation to my experimental work. My supervisor stressed the importance of exposure to as much information and culture as possible, and I saw a broad scientific spectrum from medical cases to mathematical modeling while still enjoying the city and country. Some of this information has been relevant to medical classes this year. Some of these experiences and conversations have helped me understand medicine and people better. Some of it might never be practically useful again, but it was fun to learn. My gap year was an opportunity to build on my undergraduate work, to test new realms and to add new foundations for current work and future research.

Overall, I think that a gap or deferment year is wonderful if you know how to use it. There are a couple concerns that are worth mentioning. A gap year can be daunting in its planning, execution and return. It was tough to start reading the literature of a different field: the style is different, the vocabulary is new and the background is unfamiliar. Similarly, returning to the American educational system—especially the medical system—can seem awkward. I enjoyed my gap year and my appreciation for its challenges has grown since graduation. For one year I was free to work and read as a graduate student, encouraged to travel as a tourist, able to enjoy life without a car and delighted to spend a restful working year in a city of quaint modernity.

--Arwen Long

Community Service

I made the decision to take a year off even before I began the process of applying to medical school. Here's what you can learn in one short year if you do decide to take a year off and use it wisely.

I took a year off to engage more actively in community service. I felt that the best way to spend my year off was to become a member of Notre Dame AmeriCorps. Furthermore, I saw my year of service as a test of whether I was truly ready to pursue a lifetime career of service to my community.

As the educational mentor of the AIDS Interfaith Residential Services (AIRS) in Baltimore, Maryland, I made home visits and worked with the children of low-income HIV/AIDS families. During this year with Notre Dame AmeriCorps, I changed in many ways. While most changes have been for the better, a few have been for the worse.

"You are a role model to my children," a mother said to me one day. I had only just begun spending time with her five children, and it came as a surprise to hear those words. At the same time, while such a compliment was undeserved, I felt a sense of personal gratification. More importantly, however, her words reminded me of what my grandfather had said in response to encouragement for him to retire a few years ago, "my work gives me a sustaining energy that won't leave me alone." My interactions with AIRS families reinforce the belief that my work gives me similarly "sustaining energy."

While I have had the unique opportunity to travel all around the world from the icy shores of Greenland to the remote villages of western Gambia, my experience here in Baltimore has further broadened my perspective on life. Again, I found myself far from the rolling hills of the Appalachian Mountains where I grew up. Working closely with the children of AIRS families has reminded me that, wherever one goes, children are the same. Their faces, interests and cultures may vastly differ, but their glowing smiles and ephemeral innocence are universal. Such a reminder has recently kindled an even stronger desire to work closely with children and their families, which further convinced me that I was beginning to become ready to enter the medical field.

Coupled with the recent wonderful memories of working with the children in the AIRS family program are ones of harsh and cruel reality. The children's families have gone through much turmoil and suffering in coping with not only HIV/AIDS but also other seemingly insurmountable obstacles. Many times, I felt utterly helpless, struggling to relate to their problems and to find even some small way to help. The moments of seeing tears, anger and frustration are still with me every day. In those moments, I felt a strong sense of distance and inability to relate in some way. Though I will never be able to relate to their situations, I am still obligated and compelled to continue to find whatever skills, experience and knowledge needed to improve their situations. Such obligation calls for a greater sense of responsibility and a burning desire for constant self-improvement.

Ultimately, my AmeriCorps experiences have left profound impressions upon me, compelling me to fulfill my realized goals in life. As I continue on to medical school and beyond, the road will continue not to be straight, tidy and smooth. Yet, I am convinced not only that this is truly the rightly chosen path of life but also that I am better prepared to embrace the mission of alleviating human suffering.

--Eugene Kim

Time for Yourself

Do you ever feel like you may not get into medical school? That was how I was feeling at the beginning of my senior year in college—unsure how competitive I would be in the medical school application process.

Picture this. I am on the brink of my senior college year and I had not started the application process, and I had only just completed the MCAT in August. I had tons of activities and classes scheduled for the upcoming year. And lastly, but most importantly, I had not done significant work in a hospital or lab, so who would believe I really wanted to be a doctor. All in all I felt in no way ready to enter medical school the next year, let alone hurry through the application process at that time.

So I decided to take a year off. I thought seriously about what I would do with that year. I knew it would have to be medically related or at least heavily people-oriented because my goal was to be a practicing physician. This type of activity will most likely help your application, although doing something that is not health related won't necessarily hurt. Would I want to go back to school after a year of working and making money—especially after being broke for so long. I decided that if I did not want to return to school it was better to know before I began. I worried about how I could make my year off look purposeful and legitimate as opposed to an excuse for not being ready earlier.

My choice enabled me to give whole-heartedly to the fun, work and activities of my last year in college without the additional stress of secondary applications, traveling and preparing for interviews and scholarship deadlines. And, as my senior year went on I was able to leisurely write (and rewrite) my personal statement from December until July when AMCAS started accepting applications. I was especially happy around January when senioritis reared its ugly head and settled in my mind. I was thoroughly tired of school and class and was ecstatic that I would get a year to do something completely different and relax a little. By graduation I felt like I had planned to take a year off from the beginning of college and not just from lack of preparedness for the application process.

I lived at home for my year off. It was the most financially sound decision I have made in my life thus far. I spent the summer looking for jobs, writing medical school applications and relaxing. I applied to many hospitals—most of which tech work was the only thing for which I was qualified. I applied to schools, labs and pharmaceutical companies. Eventually I accepted a position at Carolinas Medical Center working as a psychiatric technician at their Behavioral Health Center. As a tech I had joint responsibility for psychiatric in-patients on a 20-bed unit. I performed quarter or half hourly rounds assessing patients' activities of daily life, safety and well-being. On occasion I attended treatment team meetings and was asked to give input. Also, when word got out that I was applying to medical school some of the physicians invited me to sit in on some of their sessions with their patients and even see electroconvulsive shock treatment. The opportunity to observe and sit and talk with patients all day was wonderful. Psychiatric patients are a fascinating and fun population. Since I worked in a public hospital I interacted with a more impoverished subset of the population.

In addition to that day job, I worked as a hostess at a restaurant and mentored a young African American girl in foster care. Both jobs were flexible in letting me take time off for interviews, which was very important to me. From my experiences in college and on the job I had great stories to tell and considerable insight into patients' lives in the hospital. I am blessed to say I had no bad interviews nor received adverse reactions to my having taken a year off. In fact, I got encouragement for taking my time. I applied to 17 schools, accepted six interviews and was admitted to five of the institutions.

There were two additional perks to my year off. I had a lot of time to reflect on my life, read for pleasure and keep up with the news. I learned a lot about my goals and the world around me. Since I do not have as much time to do that while in medical school, I really value that period in my life.

I would recommend taking a year off to anyone who wants a break before medical school. You definitely deserve it! Just make sure you do something meaningful and worthwhile. Good luck!

--Ayaba Worjoloh

Biting the Bullet

Taking a year off isn't right for everybody. It depends on your situation. For me, it just didn't fit—here's why.

I went to undergrad here at Duke, but I was odd because I was an engineer of the biomedical persuasion. Thus, my classes were far removed from the typical pre-med fare. Memorization was nixed in favor of problem-solving and projects, and tests invariably permitted cheat sheets saturated with arcane equations. This is far different than the drinking-from-the-fire-hose-of-essential-medical-knowledge mode of learning that I knew would be necessary in medical school. I wasn't going to be doing any more traditional engineering; medical school (as perverse as it sounds) was my break from the ordinary, so to speak.

I also knew that I didn't have any particular research I wanted to undertake before medical school. The engineering project I worked on in my final two undergraduate years was quite fun and thought-provoking, but I knew I didn't want to pursue it for the remainder of my career. I wanted to become a clinician, not a basic scientist. The research I would do in medical school, even if it relates to engineering in some way, would hopefully have more of a human component.

There is also the standard "biological clock is ticking" argument. I didn't want my entire life to take place in the ivory tower (or the classroom). I wanted to become a doctor, have a family, have a brick house, raise some llamas and have a settled and happy life before I keeled over. Believe it or not, finishing one year earlier seemed to make a big difference to me in my mind.

As for charity work, I was thinking I would be more useful to the world at large after I have some medical training. There are many more medical charity projects than there are, say, engineering-based charity circuit simulation and wiring projects. Peace Corps doesn't really fit my risk-averse personality (or my physical fitness level), and I'm not so good at teaching classes. Thus, I felt like I would be more useful if I lumped a year's worth of charity into my post med school life rather than doing it right off.

So, if after four years of grueling pre-med training, you feel like all the proteins in your brain would simultaneously denature if they had to memorize one more pathway, it might be a good idea to give yourself a rest. If you are doing some exciting research that you feel you couldn't continue adequately during medical school, by all means continue. If, for any reason you feel that immediately attending medical school would prevent you from making a positive impact on people's lives, stay where you are. If you need to pay off some loans, it's fine to make a year's worth of quick bucks. Most importantly, if you're not sure med school is right for you, take time to think about your decision carefully. But, if none of these apply, go ahead, bite the bullet and enroll at the med school where you would be most happy. It isn't as horrible as they say, and you'll feel much more productive and happy with yourself if you don't loll around for a year doing nothing.

--Stanton Stebbins

Going Straight to Medical School After College

If you are trying to decide which of these paths is right for you, there are two main sets of issues to think about—the practical issues and the personal ones.

The practical

Is your application ready? Not only do you have to have all of the requirements covered (MCAT scores, required courses, recommendations), but it also makes sense to ask yourself whether the experiences you have had are sufficient to show schools that you are ready to commit yourself to working in medicine.

Research experience

Many (though not all) medical schools are research-driven, so it makes sense that they are interested in recruiting similarly-minded students. The schools ranked within the Top 10 by *U.S. News and World Report* are often among these research-driven schools, and are much more likely to admit you if you have some sort of research experience to list in your application and discuss in your interview. Furthermore, doing some sort of research will help you to decide whether or not it is something that you might be interested in doing as part or all of your career ... and you might surprise yourself! I went to Williams, a small yet research-rich liberal arts college, and it was easy to get involved with faculty research projects. I worked one summer in a chemistry lab and though the project wasn't a great fit for me, I could tell from the experience that I had a real interest in basic science research. I decided to switch labs to find work that was more interesting to me (i.e., as far away from the nuclear magnetic resonance as possible!) and ultimately decided to do a project of my own in a neuroscience lab during my senior year. It was difficult coordinating my thesis work while scrambling to finish applications and traveling for interviews, but the research project was a valuable experience for me, as well as something interesting to talk about during my interviews.

Clinical experience

If you haven't been in a hospital since you were born, it's hard to know whether you would be comfortable working with patients in a clinical setting. It's not always easy to get hands-on experience doing this, but it makes sense to do at least some sort of shadowing or observation of a working doctor before committing yourself to years of work in the wards. Some students do get hands-on experience caring for and working with patients by completing EMT training and working on an ambulance; I took the more passive and observational approach and spent a month shadowing a neurologist full-time. This experience was not enough to convince me to embrace neurology as the perfect future for me, but it helped convince me that I could enjoy working with patients in a clinical setting.

Do you want to spend senior year in college very distracted by the admissions process? This isn't trivial. Applying to med school is not going to be easy at any time in your life, but there are special things to take into consideration if you're thinking of applying during your senior year.

Academics

It doesn't matter how organized you are or how light your courseload is, trying to complete applications and go on interviews during your senior year in college will make your life somewhat of a mess. In fact, if I had fully appreciated this fact before I sent in my preliminary AMCAS application the summer before my senior year, I might have thought twice. You will be missing class, labs, and be forever indebted to your most understanding professors for letting you slide when things get out of control. If you do decide to apply during your senior year, be completely upfront with your professors when classes start and let them know that you will probably be missing class for medical school interviews—at least that way they won't be able to say you didn't warn them, and you can at least try to avoid taking classes with professors who are not going to cut you any slack.

Everything else

Know that activities and social time will be cut into as well. I had performed in several plays throughout my time at college, but my crazy interview schedule made this impossible during my senior year. In some ways, I regret not having more time to spend with my friends, enjoying the non-academic aspects of college. I'm not saying that you'll miss out on everything, but there will be sacrifices made during the application process in both the academic and non-academic parts of your life, and you should be prepared for that.

The personal

Do I really know what I really want to do? It's a simple question to ask yourself, but it can be a difficult one to answer honestly. Not only do you need sufficient experience to feel strongly that you will enjoy medicine, but you need to make sure that the motivation to attend medical school and become a physician is genuinely your own. Medical school is a long and tough road, but it will be much, much tougher and seem to last forever if you're doing it for the wrong reasons, which include the following, among others: your parents want you to go; your brother/girlfriend/cute guy in your chemistry class is going; you want to make money; or you can't think of anything else to do. For me, I can honestly say that I think practicing medicine is something that I will enjoy doing and feel good about doing, for life. If this doesn't apply to you, it might make sense to take some more time to figure out what you really want.

Are you sure that you want to do it NOW? Even if you're SURE you want to go to medical school, ask yourself whether there is something else that you'd like to do first. Once you've started school, it will be much more difficult to spend time abroad, work some random job in a coffee shop, or learn to snowboard. For me, this decision was one of the hardest to make, but I ultimately decided that there wasn't anything I felt as excited about as starting medical school the year after I graduated, and so I decided to go.

--Sarah Hart

Reapplying

I never thought that getting into medical school would be so difficult. I had been preparing myself for many years, accruing volunteer hours, participating in a variety of extracurricular activities, studying an array of subjects to make myself a well-rounded applicant, etc. I could not see myself doing anything besides medicine and I believed I could convey that easily to admissions committees. There was one factor that stood out from my profile, though; a factor I thought would be overlooked when combined with all of my other qualities. My MCAT score was only average. I had taken it twice by the time I sent in my AMCAS but it was still below what I would have liked it to be. Nonetheless, I continued the application process believing that, with the average acceptance rate to medical schools being 33 percent, I could surely get in somewhere.

With only an average MCAT score, I know now in hindsight that I should have taken deadlines more seriously and put slightly more effort into my application essays. The fall semester of my senior year was an academically difficult one, however, due to the fact that I had just declared my second major and I was taking all of the required science courses simultaneously. Thus, the applications and my future, took a backseat until after Christmas. I still managed to send in the applications on time, though I wasn't able to devote as much attention to them as I would have liked. However, I was quite confident that things were on track. I would later find out how important it is to get applications out early, as this increases the likelihood of getting early interviews. Since most schools like to fill their classes on a rolling admissions basis, early interviews can mean early acceptances. For those who fall behind, as I had, a late interview can come when most of the spots have been filled and the number of applicants for the remaining spots increases dramatically. Since I was unaware of this, I was ecstatic when I got my first and only interview in March. I came out of that interview truly believing that I would be stepping foot on that campus in the fall. However, I ended up on their waiting list and didn't realize until classes began that I had no where to go for the next year.

At this point, I should have done something to improve my MCAT score. Since it was already July, though, I decided to just go ahead and send in another AMCAS application. I felt that I had done enough in the previous year to improve my application, including working as a teaching assistant, increasing my GPA and completing an internship at Proctor and Gamble. This time, however, I was much more diligent about application turnaround. I managed to get an early interview at my alma mater, which I took to be a very positive sign. Just as with my March interview, I came out believing that I would be chosen to join the next class. Again, however, I was put in waiting list purgatory where I remained until classes began the next fall.

I was now working full-time and decided it would be best to take a year off from applying and work on that sore spot of an MCAT score. I was fortunate to have a boss who could see how passionate I was about medicine and provided me with financial support to take a review course. It was access to extensive test questions that really helped me, and I was able to improve my score by 11 points. Once I saw my score, I knew it was time to send in my third and hopefully last AMCAS. Sure enough, interviews began pouring in and I relished in traveling from school to school. I did get in to a few schools, such as my state school, but I got put on the waiting list at my top choice, Duke. So I persistently sent in letters of interest until I finally got the infamous call from the admissions secretary in June offering me a spot in the class. After three long years, and countless internal debates about whether I should choose an alternate career, I had finally made it.

If you are faced with having to reapply, my advice would be to take a step back and analyze the situation with some common sense. If you haven't made any improvements to your applications, chances are you will be rejected from the same schools again. Consider three options: first, apply to less competitive schools if you don't think you've improved your application. Second, apply to the same schools but improve upon the weak spot in your application, as I did. Third, pack it up and quit. If you're sure medicine is what you want to do, this should be the last thing on your mind.

--Dana Cairo

The Medical Scientist Training Program (MSTP)

CHAPTER 12

The MSTP—MD/PhD Program

The Medical Scientist Training Program (MSTP) is a program that supports individuals who are interesting in obtaining both the MD and PhD degrees with the intent to pursue a career in medical research. The National Institutes of Health (NIH) funds these programs in order to encourage students to become medical researchers through the completion of dual degree (MD/PhD) programs. As of 2006, there are programs at 45 institutions. Since the grants awarded to each school are reviewed every few years, the institutions that participate in the MST program may vary between years. A current list of participating schools and program can be accessed on the NIH web site (www.nih.gov; search MSTP).

All MSTP students are funded by the NIH, which covers your tuition and fees, some research-related travel and a stipend of approximately $21,000 per year (this amount varies each year). Almost all schools supplement this stipend to varying degrees. Some schools will also cover health insurance and other miscellaneous costs.

To complete the MSTP can take anywhere from six to 10 years (but if you're in the program for 10 years, somebody's going to question your commitment to getting a PhD!). The average time to complete both degrees is seven to eight years, depending on the university and the nature of your PhD. Remember, you are not limited to a PhD in the basic sciences (e.g., biology, microbiology) as long as you choose to pursue something medically related and approved by the director of your program.

There are many things to consider in choosing the right institution for your training. The two most important concerns are the quality of the medical school and the availability of departments and potential PhD advisors that attract your interest.

The MSTP Application

There is no common application for MST programs. You must apply to institutions individually, and the application and interview processes vary significantly from school to school, so be sure to check with the MSTP office at each institution to learn how each operates. The applications for MD and MSTP can be completely separate or combined to varying degrees. At most schools, you will be required to fill out a separate or additional application for the MSTP portion, as well as complete additional essays usually asking more specific questions about previous research experience. Though the AMCAS primary application does ask if you would like to pursue a dual degree, this is usually NOT the only thing that needs to be completed to be eligible for applying and interviewing with an MST program (i.e., check, check and check again what you have to do to interview for the MSTP at an individual school—they can vary widely).

Just as application processes differ between schools, interview processes will differ as well. Most MSTP interviews will entail questions regarding your research. Some schools let you decide who you would like to meet with on your interview day. Again, it would be best to inquire with the institution and check their web site about the interview process so that you can be well prepared for your interview.

MST programs are competitive to get into; many institutions receive hundreds of applications for only a few spots (usually fewer than 10 per institution per year). Overall, there are approximately 170 spots available nationwide each year. In addition to the requirements for medical school, most programs require extensive research experience to be seriously considered (more than a year of research work). Though previous publication is NOT necessary, it may be helpful in strengthening an application and gaining a competitive edge. The area of research is not as important as how seriously you pursued the research, that you demonstrated independent and original thinking, and what your professor or PI said in their letter of recommendation.

There are alternative dual degree options if an MSTP is not compatible with your personality. While these options are not funded by the NIH grant specific to the MST program, other funding may be available, and these options can be explored through the institution's graduate or medical school financial aid office. There are 75 non-MSTP MD/PhD programs offered at various institutions, and some students choose to complete the MD and PhD degrees separately from an organized program, for example by entering medical school through the traditional route and then taking a leave from medical school to complete graduate school. Alternately, some choose to pursue an MD after having fully completed their PhD or vice versa. It is also possible to do medical research after graduation with only an MD. If you do not think that a PhD is for you, there are many other dual degree programs in medical schools, including MD/JD, MD/MPH, MD/MBA, and the list goes on. Find the one that's right for you!

To obtain more info from the NIH about the program, information about MSTP can be accessed from the NIH web site. From this web site, you can access information for each program. It is also a good idea to browse through graduate program information at the schools to which you are applying.

--Malinda Boyd and Tom Petersen

The Big Decision

The decision to apply to a medical scientist training program is an initial step into a unique path. You should ask yourself the following questions: What are my career goals? What drives me? What makes me happy? Do I enjoy doing research? Would I love to teach and mentor students? Would I love to see patients and discover possible new treatments and cures for their conditions? Do I love to work hard, travel, collaborate and think? And more importantly, what the heck am I thinking?

That last question is critical. You have to know what it is you are thinking and if you are even thinking at all. If you embark on the MSTP path without resolving with yourself that therein lies your happiness and destiny, then you might be in for an unsatisfying, confusing and frustrating time. Throughout your MD/PhD training and beyond, people will ask you why you are doing it. As an aspiring MD/PhD student you will be questioned about your decision, and even discouraged from taking the MSTP route. People will ask why you are going through the rigors of MD/PhD training when MDs can become competent researchers as well. It is indeed true that MDs do become competent biomedical researchers, but having formal basic science research training is invaluable. Technical training will refine and amplify skills, and an MD/PhD degree confers access to productive collaborations, research institutions, and competitive grants which make it easier and more likely for you to be productive in biomedical research. In addition, the three to five years spent in a rigorous PhD training program endows students with the skills to design and conduct experiments, generate and interpret data, teach and present work in publications and at meetings. In essence, the time spent in a PhD program is not wasted and you graduate as a trained scientist. MD/PhDs are strategically positioned at the interface of science and medicine. This allows them to shuttle ideas from the bedside to the lab bench and vice versa. If you're interested in it, go for it and have a great time.

A key factor in evaluating one's suitability for the program is involvement in research. The research experience is an important tool by which the applicant can evaluate their own personal interest in the MSTP; it's obviously a requirement for acceptance into these programs. There is a wide misconception that the yardstick used by MSTP admission committees is the length of time the applicant has spent doing research. The actual measure used by nearly all MSTP committees is the quality of research done by the applicant. They measure your understanding of the research in which you are involved. You have to sit there and talk about your research while answering questions. You are not given a pipette and scored based on pipetting skills. No one is interested in how fast you can run a gel. The one thing that is evaluated is the depth of your understanding of your research and your research interest and passion. Certain things are required to derive satisfaction from your research experience, to convince yourself of your interest in the MSTP, and to impress your evaluators. Contrary to popular belief, these things do not include three to four years of research experience. What you need is to read and understand most of the recently published papers in your lab, and several related papers from other labs. You need a mentor who is supportive, friendly and willing to spend time with you explaining what it is that he/she does. Such a mentor might be willing to let you have your own project and steer you in the right direction; and maybe even pay for you to fly out with him/her to conferences. You need to be surrounded by graduate students who are friendly, tolerant of your presence and patient with your multiple, never-ending questions. In addition, you need to be in a lab whose work you find very interesting. To accomplish all these, I estimate that you need to be in the lab for at least nine months. If you have been in the lab for three years, that's great so long as you can show the understanding and perhaps even publications to back it up. Problems might arise if you say you have three or four years research experience and your only souvenir is that you are now the two-time heavyweight world champion in pipetting.

In my favorite lab at the University of Alabama, we studied the regulation of GABA transporters using frog eggs (xenopus laevis oocytes) as expression vectors. We used electrophysiological membrane clamp techniques and classic biochemical techniques such as the western blot, polymerase chain reaction, and radio-labeled assay experiments. I had an amazing time and everyone was very willing to show me what was going on. I also got to go to San Diego for a neuroscience meeting. It was awesome.

For prospective MD/PhD students, the decision about where to matriculate bears a lot of weight. As an MD/PhD student, you'll be in town for at least six to eight years. That's a long time to be in one place. So you want to carefully consider your options. Factors that should influence your decision might include proximity from home. It would be nice to be able to drive home on some weekends and on breaks. You might be in love with a certain person, food, music, culture or community, and hence be inclined to matriculate within certain regions of the country. Finances are also a significant consideration. Cost of living varies widely across the country as does MSTP stipend packages. It can be the difference between sharing a one bed room apartment with three roommates and living comfortably in your own newly purchased four bedroom house for the same price. You also want to consider the faculty at the institution. Their research strength, their productivity, friendliness and willingness spend time with students are very important. In particular, you want to go to a school that is strong in the areas of research you might be interested in for your PhD work. Schools do not require that you know what you will do your PhD in at the time of matriculation. In fact, at the time of matriculation, most MD/PhD students are not exactly sure where or with whom they'll be working in the PhD years. Finally, you should also consider the overall academic reputation of the institutions on your list. Several things correlate positively with institutional reputation. These include funding, strength of research, caliber of faculty and students, facilities, exposure and productivity. These are good things to have around especially for a fledgling MD/PhD matriculant who might not know exactly what it is he/she will end up studying. At a reputable school, a solid program probably exists in whatever it is that might catch your interest along the way. With that said, it is important to note that the strength of individual departments does not necessarily reflect the overall strength or reputation of the institution. Conversely, powerhouse departments exist at several universities whose overall reputation might be considered as being a notch or two below the premier universities. In addition, no one school has ongoing research in all areas of biomedical science. Therefore it is unwise to blindly jump into the most reputable school to which you are admitted.

So you apply to MSTPs, matriculate at one of them and then graduate in six to eight years, then what? There is really no such thing as a typical MD/PhD. MD/PhDs can be found in any area of biomedical research and medical practice. Common routes after graduation in order of frequency include residency programs, postdoctoral fellowships and industry. Different combinations of all three over time are also not uncommon. The residency programs that are most often chosen by MD/PhD graduates include internal medicine and pathology. Almost 100 percent of residents at some premier neurosurgery programs are MD/PhDs. This is probably due to the fact that these programs are focused on research since much remains to be learned about the brain; and people with scientific research training might be of help in uncovering some of these mysteries. There is also huge variability in how physician scientists divide up their time. Some do research exclusively and have no patient contact. Some might do exclusively clinical practice with no research. The majority do both things in some capacity. The aim of the MSTP is to bridge the gap between science and medicine so in my opinion, the ideal would be to combine both clinical practice and research in whatever proportion one finds personally suitable.

--Stephen Odaibo

Pros

On May 10th, 2002, I began to clean out my desk at the National Center for Physical Acoustics, where I had been working under Dr. Robert Hiller for two years studying a light emitting acoustical phenomenon, sonoluminesence. Dr. Hiller was darting around the lab while I copied my files from the computer. "You did some good work while you were here. I hate that you're leaving," he said. He gazed at the apparatus that we worked on together: a collage of tangled wires, spherical flasks, piezoelectric materials, bandpasses, amplifiers, laser traps and duct tape. The room was dimly lit and from the center of one of the spherical flasks a hazy blue glow could be seen emanating into the periphery. He shut down the experiment, flipping around a dozen single throw switches towards the floor. Each switch extinguished a corresponding component, and as he progressed, the flask was less alive. The last switch was more obstinate than the rest, dislodging itself from its recessed housing under the force of his thumb. The lever from the switch flew over the card table and spun in periodic precession until it landed around five feet away in Dr. Hiller's coffee mug. I blushed, I had built that part; it was fitting that it broke the day I was leaving. It was no matter to Hiller. He scratched the surface of the components affectionately. "You built most of these, didn't you?" I laughed. "Pretty obvious, isn't it?"

"I don't think I've ever had anyone break more stuff. But that's the nature of it, isn't it? Get the engraver and put your name in the corners of each of them. These are yours, your work, your contributions to the world."

In regards to science, I am a romantic. I guess I had to be to break so many things and not get discouraged. I never did though. I worked at NCPA for two years building an experiment that I never used to collect data. It took two years just to build it. Now that I'm leaving, someone else will come in and take over the experiment, probably use it to publish a paper, but that doesn't bother me at all. Looking back on that, I realized that to enjoy research, the process must be its own reward. Not to say that the work wasn't frustrating, at times it was. But any aggravation dissolved in those few moments when I realized that we were working to discover something that no one else knew.

I began to consider the MSTP 15 months previous to graduating, during the middle of my junior year at the University of Mississippi. Being a physician appealed to me, but I was reluctant to give up bench work. The MST program appeared to be a great way to achieve a research focus as a physician. The funding from the National Institute of Health was generous, allowing students to be engaged in a program that would last as long as the average MD/PhD program (seven to eight years) without becoming burdened with debt. This program, of course, had a large time commitment, one that I did not take lightly.

I had several friends vilify me when they found out how long the program was. "You're a sadist," they said. For the most part, these are the same friends that are already planning their retirement, which is telling. I can't imagine retiring. In 50 years, I hope to be the senile professor that the university slowly transitions into emeritus faculty because he won't leave. It will be hard to get rid of me. They'll have to pry the test tubes from my dead hands.

One of the investigators said something at an MSTP dinner when I first arrived at Duke that I thought was insightful. I think it is some of the best advice I have heard for someone considering entering an MD/PhD program. Those who are suited for this vocation will understand what he means. When speaking of a career in research and academic medicine, he said, "It has to be something that you enjoy, something so much a part of you that you don't think that you are fully yourself unless you are doing it."

--Mike Angelo

Cons

When I was applying to medical school, I seriously considered pursuing an MD/PhD dual degree. I had majored in chemistry, and had worked during my undergraduate years in a basic science laboratory. Research appealed to me; I enjoyed the idea of focusing my effort on one particular field of science and studying problems for which there currently were no solutions. In fact, I did think briefly about getting just the PhD degree. However, my experience volunteering in the local VA had shown me the rewards of interacting with patients in a hospital setting.

APPENDIX

Many students like this book because it provides vital statistics, admissions criteria and program descriptions for every medical school in the United States, Canada and Puerto Rico.

Essays That Will Get You into Medical School (by Daniel Kaufman, Chris Dowhan, Amy Burnham, Dan Kaufman. Barron's Educational Series: 1998)

Organized according to essay topic or personal life experience, this book can provide useful insights while you are writing your personal essay.

3. Online Resources

Association of American Medical Colleges (AAMC) (http://www.aamc.org)

The AAMC homepage provides links to official web sites concerning the Medical College Admission Test (MCAT), American Medical College Application Service (AMCAS), medical schools and more. Their MCAT web site also sells previous MCAT exams for practice.

Medical school web sites

Individual medical school web sites are the best place to obtain information about admissions requirements and application deadlines. They provide information about programs, curriculum, student life, financial aid and contact persons.

Student Doctor Network (SDN) (http://www.studentdoctor.net)

SDN is an organized collection of web sites that contain a wealth of information about applying to medical school and the field of medicine, all from the perspectives of pre-medical students, medical students and residents. Also available are chatrooms and forums where you can post your questions and concerns. Many students find the forums to be particularly helpful for getting the insider's view in the healthcare profession.

The Princeton Review Med Schools and Careers (http://www.princetonreview.com/medical)

The Princeton Review web site provides an overview of the medical school application process, tips on taking the MCAT, sources of financial aid and medical school statistics. Study courses for the MCAT are also available through Princeton Review.

Kaplan Medical (www.kaplan.com)

The Kaplan Medical program offers courses on MCAT preparation. They also have online resources on applying, financing your education and doing well in school.

4. Financial Aid Resources

Free Application for Federal Student Aid (FAFSA) (http://www.fafsa.ed.gov/)

The FAFSA web site provides application materials and deadlines for applying for federal aid.

5. Grants and Scholarships

FinAid (http://finaid.org/otheraid/medical.phtml)

Medical Help Network (http://www.medicalhelpnet.com/content/view/19/37/)

AAMC Grants and Awards (http://www.aamc.org/about/awards/start.htm)

6. Human Resources

Faculty Advisors

Your faculty advisor can be an excellent resource because he/she has followed your academic progress and is familiar with your capabilities. In fact, if you are majoring in science, particularly in the life sciences, it is likely that your faculty advisor has had some experiences with the application process because many of their advisees tend to pursue a healthcare-related profession.

Speaker Events

Sometimes your school will invite physicians, medical admissions officials, MCAT review instructors and other people intimately involved with the application process to speak to students. These speakers may be sponsored by your pre-medical advisory office, AED chapter or career services.

--Jeanne Lee and Crystal Tung

About the Authors

This Vault guide was written by 74 of the 101 students who enrolled at Duke Medical School in 2002. Class members came from 37 different states and three foreign countries. The Duke School of Medicine is located in Durham, North Carolina.